T0329392

CAMBRIDGE LIBRARY COLLECTION

Books of enduring scholarly value

North American History

This series includes accounts of historical events and movements by eye-witnesses and contemporaries, as well as landmark studies that assembled significant source materials or developed new historiographical methods. The works range from the writings of early U.S. Presidents to journals of poor European settlers, from travellers' descriptions of bustling cities and vast landscapes to critiques of racial inequality and descriptions of Native American culture under threat of annihilation. The commercial, political and social aspirations and rivalries of the 'new world' are reflected in these fascinating eighteenth- and nineteenth-century publications.

Observations on the Inhabitants, Climate, Soil, Rivers, Productions, Animals, and Other Matters Worthy of Notice

The botanist and explorer John Bartram (1699–1777) is regarded as having created the first true botanical collection in North America. Alongside Benjamin Franklin, he was also in 1743 a founding member of the American Philosophical Society. In the summer of the same year, he set out from Philadelphia on an expedition through Iroquois lands. Published in London in 1751 through the efforts of Bartram's correspondent and fellow botanist Peter Collinson, this short work chronicles the six-week journey, offering an important early insight into the region's ecology. As well as providing observations on flora, fauna and geography, Bartram includes insightful descriptions of the activities of the Native American population. The expedition members were able to travel further than was previously possible owing to the participation of the agent and interpreter Conrad Weiser, who had earned the respect of the Iroquois. The work concludes with a brief description of Niagara Falls by the naturalist Peter Kalm.

Cambridge University Press has long been a pioneer in the reissuing of out-of-print titles from its own backlist, producing digital reprints of books that are still sought after by scholars and students but could not be reprinted economically using traditional technology. The Cambridge Library Collection extends this activity to a wider range of books which are still of importance to researchers and professionals, either for the source material they contain, or as landmarks in the history of their academic discipline.

Drawing from the world-renowned collections in the Cambridge University Library and other partner libraries, and guided by the advice of experts in each subject area, Cambridge University Press is using state-of-the-art scanning machines in its own Printing House to capture the content of each book selected for inclusion. The files are processed to give a consistently clear, crisp image, and the books finished to the high quality standard for which the Press is recognised around the world. The latest print-on-demand technology ensures that the books will remain available indefinitely, and that orders for single or multiple copies can quickly be supplied.

The Cambridge Library Collection brings back to life books of enduring scholarly value (including out-of-copyright works originally issued by other publishers) across a wide range of disciplines in the humanities and social sciences and in science and technology.

Observations on the Inhabitants, Climate, Soil, Rivers, Productions, Animals, and Other Matters Worthy of Notice

Made by Mr John Bartram,
in His Travels from Pensilvania to Onondago,
Oswego and the Lake Ontario, in Canada

JOHN BARTRAM

CAMBRIDGE
UNIVERSITY PRESS

CAMBRIDGE
UNIVERSITY PRESS

University Printing House, Cambridge, CB2 8BS, United Kingdom

Cambridge University Press is part of the University of Cambridge.

It furthers the University's mission by disseminating knowledge in the pursuit of education, learning and research at the highest international levels of excellence.

www.cambridge.org
Information on this title: www.cambridge.org/9781108076449

This edition first published 1751
This digitally printed version 2015

ISBN 978-1-108-07644-9 Paperback

This book reproduces the text of the original edition. The content and language reflect the beliefs, practices and terminology of their time, and have not been updated.

Cambridge University Press wishes to make clear that the book, unless originally published by Cambridge, is not being republished by, in association or collaboration with, or with the endorsement or approval of, the original publisher or its successors in title.

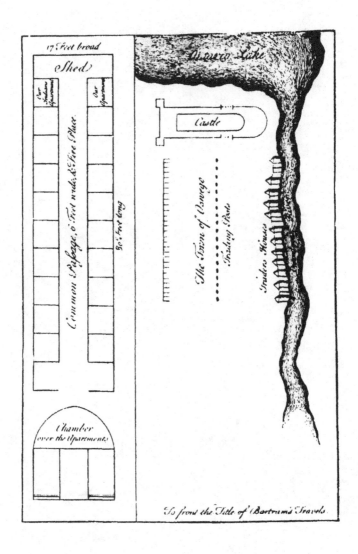

17 Feet broad

Shed

Our Trading Apartment

Our Apartment

Common Passage, 6 Feet wide, & Fire Place.

90 Feet long

Chamber over the Apartments

Muscw Lake

Castle

The Town of Oswego

Trading Posts

Traders Houses

To front the Title of Bartram's Travels.

OBSERVATIONS

ON THE

*Inhabitants, Climate, Soil, Rivers, Productions,
Animals,* and other matters worthy of Notice.

MADE BY

Mr. JOHN BARTRAM,

In his Travels from

PENSILVANIA

TO

ONONDAGO, OSWEGO and the Lake ONTARIO,

In *CANADA.*

To which is annex'd, a curious Account of the

CATARACTS at *NIAGARA.*

By Mr. PETER KALM,

A *Swedish* GENTLEMAN who travelled there.

LONDON.
Printed for J. WHISTON and B. WHITE, in
Fleet-Street, 1751.

OBSERVATIONS

MADE BY

Mr. *JOHN BARTRAM,*

In his Journey from

Penſilvania to *Onondago,* &c.

THE 3d of *July* 1743, I ſet out from my houſe on *Skuylkil River,* with *Lewis Evans,* and travelled beyond *Perkiomy Creek* the firſt day. The weather was exceeding hot. The 4*th,* we ſet out before day, and ſtopp'd at *Marcus Hulin*'s by *Manatony;* then croſſed *Skuylkil,* and rode along the weſt ſide over rich bottoms, after which we aſcended the *Flying Hill,* (ſo called from the great number of wild Turkeys that uſed to fly from them to the plains) here we had a fine proſpect of the *Blue Mountains,* and over the rich *Vale of Tulpehocken;* the deſcent into which is ſteep and ſtoney. Through this vale we travelled

weſt,

weſt, and by the way obſerved a large ſpring
16 feet deep, and above 20 yards wide, which
iſſued out of a limeſtone rock, the ground
about it pretty level, deſcending gradually
towards the ſpring which ran eaſtward. At
at night we lodged at *Conrad Weiſers*, who
is the general Interpreter, and who went with
us; his buſineſs was to ſettle an affair with the
Indians at *Onondago*.

The 5*th*, We croſſed *Tulpehocken Creek*
which runs eaſt, and emptieth itſelf into
Skuylkil, and a little after a ſmall branch of
Swataro which runs Weſt into *Suſquehanah*.
Theſe two large creeks receive moſt of the
water of that great rich vale between the
Flying Hills and *Tulpehocken Hill*, from which
the vale and creek receive their names, and
is itſelf ſo called from the *Indian* word ſigni-
fying a tortoiſe, unto which the natives of
the country have conceived it bears ſome ſimi-
litude. And theſe two hills are the ſouthern
boundary of this fine limeſtone vale, many
hundred miles long, and from 10 to 20 miles
broad to the northern boundary formed by the
Great Blue Mountains.

Having called on a man who was to go
with us and carry part of our proviſions to
Shamokin, he could not get his horſe ſhod
that day, but we rode to *William Parſons's*
plantation, who received and entertained us
very

very kindly; his house is about six miles from the *Blue Mountains*.

The 6*th*, we set forward and ascended the first *Blue ridge*, from the top of which we made an observation, *Conrad Weifers Hill* bearing south 20 degrees east, the northern prospect to two gaps, thro which we were to pass to the *North Hill*, N. 30 deg. W about 10 miles distant. The top and south side of this ridge is midling land, half a quarter of a mile broad, and produced some wild grass, abundance of fern, oak and chesnut trees. Descending the North side we found it more poor, steep and stony, and came soon to the first branch of *Swataro* which runs between the ridges, and is 3 miles from the next branch, all very poor land; but on this second branch it is good low land, with large trees of 5 leaved white pine, poplar, and white oak, here we dined by a spruce swamp.

After dinner we passed the openings of two ridges, the last of which was by the bank of the principal branch of *Swataro*, the soil poor and stoney; then we ascended a great ridge about a mile steep, and terribly stoney most of the way: near the top is a fine tho' small spring of good water. At this place we were warned by a well known alarm to keep our distance from an enraged rattle snake that had put himself into a coiled posture of defence, within a dozen yards of our path, but

we

we punifhed his rage by ftriking him dead on
the fpot: he had been highly irritated by
an *Indian* dog that barked eagerly at him, but
was cunning enough to keep out of his reach,
or nimble enough to avoid the fnake when he
fprung at him. We took notice that while
provoked, he contracted the mufcles of his
fcales fo as to appear very bright and fhining,
but after the mortal ftroke, his fplendor became much diminifhed, this is likewife the
cafe of many of our fnakes.

The north fide of the Hill is not fo ftony as
the fouth, but yet very poor. Thence we
traveled 7 miles over feveral hollows, fwamps
and fmall ridges, full of fcrubby bufhes,
and ftill poor and ftoney to the laft great
ridge, which is compofed chiefly of large
gravel, as big as pidgeons or pullets eggs, and
even the rocks feemed but heaps of the fame
materials; the defcent on the north fide is very
fteepand rocky, large craggy rocks are difpofed
on all fides, moft part of the way down, which
brought us to a fine vale, where we lodged by
a creek called *Saurel*, and were grievoufly
ftung all night with fmall gnats, fo that I flept
very little.

The *7th*, we fet out weft from *Saurel* creek
and traveled down the vale, which is pretty
good land: and leaving the creek, foon croffed
another runing along the north fide of the vale,
by the bank of which we rode through a grove
of

of white Pine, very lofty aud fo clofe, that the Sun could hardly fhine through; at the end of this the two branches joined. Riding a little farther, we paffed through a gap of a moderate hill, north by the creek fide, where we found a fifhing place, moftly a deep hole near a rock; there we went weft on the north fide of the creek, and dined at what is called the *Double Eagle*. The land hereabouts is middling white oak and huckleberry land, and by the creek fide pretty good wild grafs, and the 3d branch enters about 30 rood below; having croffed this, we went up a vale of middling foil, covered with high oak Timber, nearly weft to the top of the hill, (moft of the way being a white clay under a fhallow furface), where we firft obferved the impreffion of fhells in fome of the loofe ftones, and from whence we had a fair profpect of the river *Sufquehanah*.

The defcent from hence foon brought us to *Mohony*, our lodging for this night. Here the foil is very good throughout the neck, formed by the river and the creek, which is about 3 poles wide. It rained this night through our old, tho' newly erected lodging, which was an *Indian Cabin* that we took the liberty to remove, knowing they ufually leave behind them a good ftock of fleas on the ground they inhabit; however, the wet deprived me of my

rest

rest that I had taken so much pains to secure
against the vermin.

July 8. We crossed the creek and rode along a
rich bottom near the river for two miles, producing most kinds of our forest trees, and a
large species of *Scutelaria* two feet high :
thence along the river side, near a mile N. 20
deg. E. to the foot of a fertile hill, where
leaving the river, our way N. E. through
several narrow valleys and over small hills,
generally middling land, yielding oak, hickery,
chesnut, and some pine, to the summit of a
high hill, where we saw *Shamokin Hill*, distant four miles only ; going down we came
to uneven stony ground producing pitch pine
and oak, as far as the point of *Shamokin Hill*,
whence we had a pleasant prospect of the fall
of the river, quite cross without any great
Rocks. The stream runs very swift, but
canoes or flat-bottomed boats may go up or
down well enough : the bottom of this descent is washed by *Shamokin Creek* three rods
wide , this we forded to a fruitful bottom half
a mile wide, beyond which, two miles good
oak land brought us to the town of *Shamokin*. It contains eight cabbins near the river's
bank right opposite the mouth of the west
branch that interlocks with the branches of
Allegheny. It is by means of this neighbourhood that we may reasonably hope, when
these parts shall be better known, that a very
beneficial

beneficial Trade may be extended through the *Hokio* into the *Miffiffippi* and its branches among the numerous nations that inhabit their banks. It were to be wifhed, that the *Englifh* government in thefe parts had been more diligent in fearching and furveying the heads of their own rivers and the fources of the others that run weftwards from the backs of their refpective provinces. Yet enough is already known to juftify the furmifes of *Mr. de la Sale*, who in his Journal addreffed to the *Count de Frontenac* expreffes his fears, left the *Englifh*, from their fettlements, fhould poffefs themfelves of the trade on the *Miffiffippi*. I quartered in a trader's cabbin, and about midnight the *Indians* came and called up him and his fquaw, who lay in a feparate part where the goods were depofited, whether together or no I did not ask. She fold the *Indians* rum, with which being quickly intoxicated, men and woman began firft to fing and then dance round the fire; then the women would run out to other cabbins and foon return, leaving the men finging and dancing the war dance, which continued all the next day. An *Englifhman* when very drunk will fall faft afleep for the moft part, but an *Indian*, when merry, falls to dancing, running, and fhouting, which violent action probably may difperfe the fumes of the liquor, that had he fat ftill or remained quiet, might have made

made him drowſy, and which is even carries off by continued agitation.

As ſoon as we alighted they·ſhewed us where to lay our baggage, and then brought us a bowl of boiled ſquaſhes cold ; this I then thought poor entertainment, but before I came back I had learnt not to deſpiſe good *Indian* food. This hoſpitality is agreeable to the honeſt ſimplicity of antient times, and is ſo punctually adhered to, that not only what is already dreſſed is immediately ſet before a traveller, but the moſt preſſing buſineſs is poſtponed to prepare the beſt they can get for him, keeping it as a maxim that he muſt always be hungry, of this we found the good effects in the fleſh and bread they got ready for us.

July 9. After breakfaſt *Lewis Evans* and myſelf went to the point of the mountain cloſe to the N. E. branch, a mile and half up the river from our lodging, and good level rich land all the way ; we walked thither, carrying our blankets with us, and ſlept near three hours. Here we regulated our journey, and having taken a pleaſant view of the range of mountains, and the charming plane of *Shamokin*, 2 miles long and above one broad, skirted on the Weſt and North by the river, and encompaſſed Eaſt, and partly South, with lofty hills, beſides a fine vale bordering the North Weſt branch, we returned to the town and dined. In the

afternoon

afternoon. In the afternoon we borrowed a canoe, and paddled up the Weſt branch. It is near two-thirds as broad as the North Eaſt or main river : I went aſhore on the ſouth ſide to the point of a hill to look for curioſities, but found none ; the rock conſiſted of a dark coloured ſhelly ſtone. Then we diverted our ſelves with ſwimming, the water was chin deep moſt of the breadth, and ſo clear one might have ſeen a pin at the bottom. At night I hung up my blanket like a hammock, that I might lie out of the reach of the fleas, troubleſome and conſtant gueſts in an *Indian* hut ; but I found my contrivance too cool for a place open on all ſides, tho covered with a kind of granary, eſpecially the wind blowing cold from the N. W.

10. We departed in the morning with *Shickcalamy* and his ſon, he being the chief man in the town, which conſiſted of *Delaware Indians*, he was of the ſix nations, or rather a *Frenchman*, born at *Mont-real,* and adopted by the *Oneidoes*, after being taken priſoner ; but his ſon told me he was of the *Cayuga* nation, that of his mother, agreeable to the *Indian* rule *Partus ſequitur ventrem,* which is as reaſonable among them as among cattle, ſince the whole burthen of bringing up falls on her ; therefore in caſe of ſeparation the children fall to her ſhare.

D   We

We had many advantages from the company of thefe guides, were perfectly acquainted with that part of the country, and being of the fix Nations they were both a credit and protection ; and, alfo as we went to accommodate the differences, and allay the Heart-burnings that had been raifed by a late skirmifh on the back of *Virginia*, between fome of thefe nations and the *Englifh*, we could not but derive a confidence from the company of a chief.

We coafted the river near a mile to the ford, where we had a good bottom not above 3 feet deep ; this brought us to an Ifland near 2 miles long and a quarter broad, pretty rich at the lower end, and near the river, but the higher end fandy, from the drift left there by the floods, it therefore produces little but *pitch pine*. After leaving the lower end where we faw feveral cabbins, we once more took water for the oppofite fhore, but the bottom is lefs even, though not above half as wide as the laft, which is about 400 yards.

Hence leaving the weft branch about half a mile on our left, and rich low ground between with gravel, oak and pitch-pine land on our right, we reached a pretty fpring of good water, fituated between the fwamp and dry ground. This, fince our paffage over the *Blue Mountains*, was the only one we met with till we came near *Onondago*, for on that fide

side the currents and creeks are chiefly formed
by the water ousing and draining from the
bottoms of the mountains and hills, and are
gradually collected in this manner into rivu-
lets But on the south of this great ridge, it
gushes out between the rocks in streams
big enough to turn a mill, in other places
rising and bubbling out of the earth in quantity sufficient to fill a pipe an inch square, or
thereabouts.

Our journey now lay through very rich
bottoms to a creek 6 miles from *Shamokin*, a
great extent of fruitful low ground still con-
tinuing. Here we found a fine meadow of
grafs on our right, and rich dry ground on
the left. In our path lay a large Rattle-
snake, but he civilly crept into the grass, and
let us pass by without danger. Our way from
hence lay through an old *Indian* field of excellent soil, where there had been a town, the
principal footsteps of which are peach-trees,
plumbs and excellent grapes. A great flood
came down this branch a few years past, and
drove abundance of sand over this ground a
great depth among the trees. It rose 20 feet
perpendicular, washing away many yards of
the bank, which was composed of gravel and
sand, and doubtless had been raised to that
heighth by former inundations, for the wood
ground 30 rod from the river is several feet

lower

lower than the bank ; a little above this deva-
ftation we dined.

And now leaving the river we held a new
courfe over a fine level, then down a rich
hollow to a *run*, where we faw a fummer
duck ; and fo down the *run*, a little beyond
this turns a path to *Wiomick*, a town on
the eaft branch, hence N. N. E. then N. after
W. to a rich bottom near the river, where
Shickcalamy formerly dwelt, at the upper end
of which refiftlefs torrents had carried abundance of fand into the woods. With this bottom we left the river for the prefent, and kept
a variable courfe through the gap of the
mountain N. and N. W. over middling cham-
pion land, producing fome pitch pine, and
large white and black oak, fome fwamps and
brooks, by one of which we lodged in a
fertile valley, that we reached before night.

11. About break of day it began to rain,
and the *Indians* made us a covering of bark
got after this manner : They cut the tree
round through the bark near the root, and
make the like incifion above 7 feet above
it , thefe horizontal ones are joined by a
perpendicular cut, on each fide of which they
after loofen the bark from the wood, and
hewing a pole at the fmall end, gradually ta-
pering like a wedge about 2 feet, they force
it in till they have compleated the fepara-
tion all round, and the bark parts whole
from

from the tree, one of which, a foot diameter, yields a piece 7 feet long and above
3 wide : And having now prepared four forked
sticks, they are set into the ground the longer
in front; on these they lay the cross-poles,
and on them the bark. This makes a good
tight shelter in warm weather. The rain was
quickly over, but as it continued cloudy, we
did not care to leave our shed. Here our *Indians* shot a young deer, that afforded us a
good feast.

12. We set forward and travelled up the
Run, bearing N. W. along a narrow valley,
moderately rich, the hills hung with lofty
timber, the stones generally flat, then up a steep
hill, where I found fossil steel in many stones,
the soil middling oak land; and here had a
view of a Bluf point N. by the river side;
then descending down a steep hill N. E. we
came to a rich bottom by the river; hence N.
after N. W. to a creek, and so through a grove
of white walnut and locust, and exceeding. rich
land, half a mile broad, and now some higher
level land, affording oak, hickery, walnut, locust,
and pitch pine, our course generally N. N. W.
till riding over a hazel plane we met eight
Shawanese Indians on horseback coming from
Allegheny, and going to *Wiomick* upon an important account, as they said. We turned
back with them to the adjacent wood, and
sate down together under a shady oak; the

squaw

fquaw which they brought to wait upon them kindled a fire to light their pipes ; our Interpreter and *Shickcalamy* fet down with them to fmoke, the cuftomary civility when two parties meet ; *Conrad Weifar* underftanding they were fome of the chiefs of the *Shawanefe*, acquainted them with our bufinefs at *Onondago*, a compliment they were fo well pleafed with, that they gave us the *Tohay*, a particular *Indian* expreffion of approbation, and which is very difficult for a white man to imitate well , after half an hour's grave difcourfe feveral of them went to catch the horfes, and one of the principal men made a handfome fpeech, with a pleafant well compofed countenance, to our interpreter, to the following effect : ' That they were fenfible with what ' an unwearied diligence he had hitherto been ' inftrumental in preferving peace and good ' harmony between the *Indians* and *White* ' *People*, and that as they could not but now ' commend the prudence and zeal with which ' he had effected this laudable purpofe, fo ' they earneftly entreated and fincerely hoped ' he would ftill perfevere in the fame endea- ' vours and with the fame fuccefs, and that his ' good offices may never be wanting on any ' future occafion.

The *Shawanefe*, or *Shaounons*, as they are called by the *French*, are the fame people, the *Six* nations : and at *New York* are called *Satanas* ;

they

they dwell upon the *Hokio* and to the southward of it, between whom and that of the *Cherokees* is a river sometimes called by that name. It was against this people the six nations first turned their Arms with success, after they had fled before warlike *Adarondacks*, and having thus learn'd to conquer, ventured to attack their hitherto victorious enemies, who could not have supported this war without the unexpected assistance they received from the *French*.

After taking our leaves, we continued our journey to a large creek 4 or 5 rod wide which washes on each shore a charming country of rare soil as far as the river. On the other side of this creek we rode through a deserted Town in the neck between them; a few miles more brought us to our dining place, and in the afternoon we turned our backs on this branch, and rode N. W. down a valley 20 rods wide, wooded with pitch pine on the right hand and white on the left, the *Run* between; then N. W. by W. by the side of a hill and bottom of white pine, down which we rode 2 hours, upon better land, the N. W. middling land, now up a hill N. W. to a point, a prospect of an opening bearing N. then down the hill to run, and over a rich neck lying between it and *Tiadaughton* bearing N. W. where we lodged within about 50 yards of a hunting cabin, where there were 2 Men, a Squaw and a child,

child, the men came to our fire and made us a
prefent of fome venifon, and invited Mr *Weifar*,
Shickalamy and his fon, to a feaft at their cabin.
It is incumbent on thofe who partake of a feaft
of this fort, to eat all that comes to their
fhare or burn it: now *Weifar* being a traveller
was intitled to a double fhare, but he being
not very well, was forced to take the benefit of a
liberty indulged him, of eating by proxy,
and called me, but both being unable to cope
with it, *Lewis* came in to our affiftance, not-
withftanding which we were hard fet to get
down the neck and throat, for thefe were
allotted us; and now we had experienced the
utmoft bounds of their indulgence, for *Lewis*
ignorant of the ceremony of throwing the
bone to the dog, tho' hungry Dogs are generally nimble, the *Indian* more nimble, laid
hold of it firft, and committed it to the fire,
religioufly covering it over with hot afhes.
This feems to be a kind of offering, perhaps
firft fruits to the Almighty power to crave
future fuccefs in the approaching hunting fea-
fon, and was celebrated with as much decency
and more filence, than many fuperftitious ce-
remonies: the bigotry of the popifh miffionaries tempt them to compafs fea and land to
teach their weak Profelites what they call the
chriftian religion. To this I may add another
ceremony at bear hunting, as related by a
celebrated author, this diverfion being in the
winter,

winter, when this animal is very fat, the greafe
that fwims on the broth becomes a perfect oil,
which the *Indians* frequently drink untill
they burft —— As foon as the bear is
killed, the hunter places the fmall end of
his pipe in its mouth, and by blowing in
the bowls, fills the mouth and throat full of
fmoak, then he conjures the departed Spirit
not to refent the injury done his body, nor to
thwart his future fport in hunting, but as he
receives·no anfwer to this, in order to know
if his prayers have prevailed, he cuts the liga-
ment under the bear's tongue, if thefe ligaments
contract and fhrivel up, being caft into the
fire, which is done with great folemnity and
abundance of invocations : then it is efteemed a
certain mark (as it rarely fails) that the *manes*
are appeafed. It was now time to return to
our fire where we laid us down to reft.

The 13*th*, in the morning, the *Indians* re-
paid our vifit, and entertained us with a fa-
miliar converfation for half an hour at the fire.
We then fet out up the creek, where I obferved
three noble white pine trees, with many large
green cones hanging on the top and fide branches
over the creek, which was three rods broad and
pretty deep, had thefe been ripe I know not
how we fhould have got at them, as they
were at the extremity of large branches, that
hung over the Water, on which part of the
branch they generally grow. Soon after we

E   came

came to a spacious level of midling land,
oak, and pine, next to a large rich bottom,
and at the upper end o an extensive grove of
white pine, after this a grassy plain of 20 acres,
then round the end of a hill, and along a valley, and run N. by W. high timber and good
land on the hill side N. then W. and lastly, at
half an hour after 8 N. here our *Indians* shot 2
young deer. The land and timber good, brown
soil, and the stones flat and gritty. From
hence going over a hill we saw a gap N. N.W.
and descending down a steep part of the hill
to the head of a stoney brook and hollow,
we made our way through it, it was full of
spruce and white pine; at the bottom we
killed a rattle snake, then crossed the brook
and traversed a rich bottom N. N. E. the
upper end pine, spruce, oak, laurel, poplar
and chesnut, some limes, stoney and brown
soil, several times crossed the creek and over
rich bottoms and stoney hill sides with laurel,
pine, spruce and swamps, till towards night.
On the north side of a deep stoney yet rich
soil, I found roots of *Ginseng*; at night we
lodged by a creek, and the two *Indians* that
feasted with us, who accompanied us to the
Cayuga branch.

The 14*th*, Having forded the creek we
kept generally a N. N. E. course, mostly along
rich bottoms interspersed with large spruce
and white pine, oak, beach and plane tree,

ginseng,

ginfeng, and many more. We frequently paffed
the creek (which was very ftrong) for the
mountains often clos'd on one fide; it was big
enough to turn two mills. At 9 o'clock the
Indians fifhed for trout, but caught none, being provided with no other means of taking
them but by poles fharpened at the end to
ftrike them, and the water deep: at the foot
of a hill we croffed the creek once more, and
rode along a fine bottom, full of great wild
nettles. The timber was fugar birch, fugar
maples, oak and poplar, our courfe N. W.
continued till after 12 'clock, then followed
the eaft branch N. N. E. about a mile, all a
rich bottom where we found a *Liching Pond*,
where we dined, the backs parts of our country are full of thefe liching ponds, fome are
of black fulphureous mud, fome of pale clay,
the deer and elks are fond of licking this clay,
fo that the pond becomes enlarged to a rood or
half an acre, the foil, I fuppofe contains fome
faline particles agreeable to the deer, who
come many miles to one of thefe places, there
had been a great elk there that morning, but
the *Indians* told us that many years ago fome
Indians quarrelled there, in the fquable one
loft his life, and that this made the deer keep
from thence for many years.

Now traveling up the run eaft, we left it on
the right hand, to go up a hill covered with
fpruce, oak fpruce, lawrel, opulus, yew; with

E 2   ginfeng

ginfeng and ataliafhum in abundance, then kept generally an eaft courfe, having feveral hollows and fteep afcents and over many boggy rotten places, fome laurel and very high timber, then down the fide of a hill to an old beaver dam, over which we paffed, and then over a large level of very good ground, tall timber and abundance of leather-bark or *thymelea*, which is plentiful in all this part of the country. Our lodging was in this fpacious flat.

The 15th, We fet out a N. E. courfe, and paffed by very thick and tall timber of beach, chefnut, linden afh, great magnolia, fugar-birch, fugar-maple, poplar, fpruce and fome white pine, with ginfeng and maidenhair; the foil black on the furface, and brown underneath, the ftones a brown grit, the way very uneven over fallen trees, abundance of hollows, and heaps of earth, turned up by the roots of proftrate timber : hence it is that the furface is principally compofed of rotten trees, roots, and mofs, perpetually fhaded, and for the moft part wet, what falls is conftantly rotting and rendring the earth loofe and fpungy; this tempts abundance of yellow wafps to breed in it, which were very troublefome to us throughout our journey, on the branches of *Sufquehanah* our courfe this day was generally eaft, and we got through this difmal wildernefs about two hours before funfet, and
came

came to oak and hickery land, then down a
fteep hill producing white pine to a creek called
Conuria a branch of *Towintohow*, where we
lodged in a bottom producing ginfeng, farea-
parilla mediola, maidenhair, darallia, panax,
mitela, chriftophoriana, with white, red and
blue berries, we had a fine warm night, and
one of the *Indians* that had fo generoufly
feafted us, fung in a folemn harmonious manner, for feven or eight minutes, very different
from the common *Indian* tune, from whence
I conjectured it to be a hymn to the great
fpirit as they exprefs it. In the morning I
asked the Interpreter what the *Indian* meant
by it, but he did not hear him, and indeed I
believe none of the company heard him but
myfelf, who wake with a little noife, rarely
fleeping found abroad.

The 16*th*, We began our journey up a little
hill, fteep and fomewhat ftoney, and then
through oak, chefnut, huckleberries, and
honeyfuckles, the land poor, fometimes white
pine, fpruce and lawrel; thus far N. but at
half an our after feven N. E. through a great
white pine, fpruce fwamp full of roots, and
abundance of old trees lying on the ground,
or leaning againft live ones, they ftood fo
thick that we concluded it almoft impoffible
to fhoot a man at 100 yards diftant, let him
ftand never fo fair. The ftraight bodies of
thefe trees ftood fo thick, a bullet muft hit
one before it could fly 100 yards, in the moft
open

open part. At half an hour after nine, we rode
down a small hill, and crossed a small run,
then climb'd a steep hill of oak land, and by
ten to a large creek called *Uskoho*, then round
the point of a hill, midling land, and up
the side thereof which was good, and
down the other side very steep to a *Run*,
with good corn land to the top of a hill in
sight of the east branch of *Susquehanah*, so far
we had pale clay land from the wilderness,
though blackish on the surface, for 2, 3 or 4
inches, then down half a mile on a moderate
descent, good oak and hickery land to a large
rich grassy and weedy bottom, 40 rood wide,
producing elm; birch, linden, lotus, white-
walnut, and very large white pine, where the
land is a little higher than common; at the
upper end of this bottom we dined at half an
hour after 12, we set out again at 3, course N.
along a steep hill side, full of excellent flat
whet-stones of all sizes, from half a foot, to 4
feet long, and from 2 inches to a foot wide,
and from half an inch to a foot thick; I brought
one home which I have used to whet my ax,
scythe, chizzels and knife, and is yet very little
the worse for wear, it is as fine as the *English*
rag, but of a blackish colour: this lasted two
miles close to the river which is here 100 yards
wide, and deep enough for flat-bottomed boats,
then we came to a very rich low land, most of
the way N. N. E. to the *Cayaga* branch, near
100 yards wide which we crossed, then rode

near

near a mile to the town-houfe, bearing **N.** this
town is called *Tohicon*, and lies in a rich neck
between the branch and main river: the *Indians*
welcomed us by beating their drum, as foon as
they faw us over the branch, and continued
beating after the *Englifh* manner as we rode to
the houfe, and while we unfaddled our Horfes,
laid in our luggage and entered our felves: the
Houfe is about 30 foot long, and the fineft
of any I faw among them. The *Indians* cut
long grafs and laid it on the floor for us to fit
or lie on ; feveral of them came and fat down
and fmoaked their pipes, one of which was
fix foot long, the head of ftone, the ftem a
reed, after this they brought victuals in the
ufual manner: here I obferved for the firft
time in this journey, that the worms which
had done much mifchief in feveral parts of our
Province, by deftroying the grafs and even
corn for two fummers, had done the fame thing
here, and had eat off the blade of their maize
and long white grafs, fo that the ftems of both
ftood naked 4 foot high; I faw fome of the
naked dark coloured grubs half an inch long,
tho' moft of them were gone, yet I could
perceive they were the fame that had vifited
us two months before; they clear all the grafs
in their way, in any meadow they get into,
and feem to be periodical as the locufts and
caterpillar, the latter of which I am afraid
will do us a great deal of mifchief next fummer. Here one of our hofts at the hunting
cabin

cabin left us to go up this branch to his own country, that of the *Cayagas*, this night it rained a little, and the morning was very foggy.

17*th.* Day, we croſſed the neck to the eaſt branch of *Suſquehanah*, up which we travelled along a rich bottom of high graſs and woods of a fine creek, then over oak and pitch pine land to a ſwampy run and fine meadow ground, then eaſt through white and pitch pine, oak, hickery and hazel bottom, and ſo N. E. to the river, where grew a white pine cloſe to the water, with four green cones on, ſtill we kept N. E. at 10 bore S. Here the river turned thus, occaſioned by ſome high barren mountains on the other ſide, whoſe ſides came cloſe to it, and turned the ſtream in this crooked manner. We travelled through a fine vale of pine land. Here was a place where the *Indians* had been a *pawawing*. They cut a parcel of poles, which they ſtick in the ground in a circle, about the bigneſs of hop poles, the cicrle about five foot diameter, and then bring them together at the top, and tie them in form of an * oven, where the conjurer placeth himſelf; then his aſſiſtants cover the cage over cloſe with blankets and to make it ſtill more ſuffocating, hot ſtones are rolled in; after all this the prieſt muſt cry aloud, and agitate

his

---

* Vide Capt. *Beverley's* hiſt. of *Virginia*, 8*vo.* a curious and uſeful work, and the Baron *Lahontan's* entertaining voyages in theſe parts.

his body after the moſt violent manner, till
nature has almoſt loſt all her faculties before
the ſtubborn ſpirit will become viſible to him,
which they ſay is generally in the ſhape of
ſome bird. There is uſually a ſtake drove into
the ground about four foot high and painted.
I ſuppoſe this they deſign for the *winged airy
Being* to perch upon, while he reveals to the
invocant what he has taken ſo much pains to
know. However, I find different nations
have different ways of obtaining the pretended
information. Some have a bowl of water,
into which they often look, when their
ſtrength is almoſt exhauſted, and their ſenſes
failing, to ſee whether the ſpirit is ready to
anſwer their demands. I have ſeen many of
theſe places in my travels. They differ from
their ſweating coops, in that they are often
far from water, and have a ſtake by the cage,
yet both have a heap of red hot ſtones put in.
at 11 we dreſſed our dinner, and found an
Indian by the river ſide, reſting himſelf; all
his proviſion was a dried eel ; this he made us
a preſent of, and we gave him a ſhare of our
dinner. Their way of roaſting eels is thus ;
they cut a ſtick about three foot long, and as
thick as one's thumb, they ſplit it about a
foot down, and when the eel is gutted, they
coil it between the two ſides of the ſtick,
and bind the top cloſe, which keeps the eel
flat, and then ſtick one end in the ground before a good fire.

F   At

At half an hour after one we set out, middling oak land but stony, yet no great rocks; at 2 N. E. then N. good land, a rich bottom and flat stones on rising ground; we crossed the *Owagan* branch about thirty yards wide. Then half a mile to the town so called, where we lodged, there is very good land in this neck between the branch and main river. A little before sun-set I walked out of town to regulate my journal; but the gnats were so troublesome I could not rest a minute. They bit my hands so cruelly I was forced to give over my purpose. These are so troublesome from sun-rising to sun-setting that we could not rest while we were eating our victuals without making several fires of wet leaves round us to keep them off.

18. This morning we sent an *Indian* with a string of Wampum to *Onondago*, to acquaint them with our coming, and the business we came about, that they might send messengers to the several nations to hasten their deputies to meet them as soon as possible, for this town serves the five nations as *Baden* does the thirteen cantons of *Switzerland*, with this difference, that *Onondago* is at the same time the capital of a canton.

We set out at half an hour after 9, and travelled till 6; this day our general course was N. and N. W. having fine level rich land most of the way, and tall timber oak, birch, beech

beech, afh, fpruce, linden, elm and herb
hierophilon, hepatica and maidenhair in abundance. We lodged by *Front Creek* in a fpa-
tious vale, and it looking like rain, we made
us a cabbin of fpruce bark, but no rain
came.

19. We rode over good level land : after
we came to very fwampy bottoms, thickets
and hills of fpruce, and white pine ; here
were three ridges of fteep hills that run nearly
E. and W. and with difficulty we rode over
their fteep cliffs, which projected clofe to the
creek. We were feveral times obliged to
ford it backwards and forwards. Several runs
come into the creek on both fides from between the mountains, Now we came to moft
excellent level ground, than which nothing
can be more fruitful, full of tall timber, fugar,
maple, birch, linden, afh, and beech, and
fhrubs, as opulus, green maple, hornbeam,
hama m elis, folanum, goofterries and red cur-
rans triphilum in abundance. Here we dined
by a pleafant creek and choice land. After
dinner we foon began to mount up a pretty
fteep hill, covered with oak, birch, afh, and
higher up abundance of chefnut and fome
hickery. This is middling land, the produce
the fame for three miles as our land bears
with us. It lies very high, and when cleared
will have an extenfive profpect of fertile
vales on all fides. We then rode down a long

F 2   rich

rich hill of moderate defcent, where grew abundance of goofeberries, all the trees were crouded with wild pigeons, which, I fuppofe, breed in thefe lofty fhady trees. I found many foffils on this hill.

Another fertile valley welcomed us at the bottom, over which travelling a mile we lodged at a *Run*, which our *Indians* told us emptied into the lake *Ontario*; if fo, it muft run into the *Cayuga* river, and fo to *Ofwego*.

20. We continued our journey in this pleafant vale until we afcended a hill, beyond which a flant brought us to two ponds that run into a branch of *Sufquehanah*; croffing this we joined a part from the *Carugas* country; then over a rich level to another branch big enough to turn a mill where we croffed it. It was now three-quarters after 10, then good land to half an hour after 12 yet no hickery nor oak, but elm, fugar, maple, beech, birch, white walnuts, hop, hornbeam, and abundance of ginfeng. After dinner we paffed a branch of the great *Sufquehanah*, down which lake canoes may go quite to where the river is navigable for boats. On the banks I found the *gale* like the *European*. This is the neareft branch of *Sufquehanah* river to that of *Onondago*. Leaving this on our right, on our left we perceived a hill, where the *Indians* fay *Indian* corn, tobacco and fquafhes were found on the following occafion :

cafion : An *Indian* (*whofe wife had eloped*)
came hither to hunt, and with his skins to
purchafe another here, he efpied a young
fquaw alone at the hill ; going to her, and
enquiring where fhe came from, he received
for anfwer, that fhe came from heaven to
provide fuftenance for the poor *Indians*, and
if he came to that place twelve months
after he fhould find food there. He came
accordingly and found corn, fquafhes and tobacco, which were propagated from thence
and fpread through the country, and this filly
ftory is religioufly held for truth among them.
Our way hence, lay over fine rich level land
as before, but when we left it, we enter'd a
miferable thicket of fpruce, opulus, and dwarf
yew, then over a branch of *Sufquehanah*, big
enough to turn a mill, came to ground as
good as that on the other fide the thicket ;
well cloathed with tall timber of fugar birch,
fugar maple, and elm. In the afternoon it
thunder'd hard pretty near us, but rained little :
We obferved the tops of the trees to be fo clofe
to one another for many miles together, that
there is no feeing which way the clouds drive,
nor which way the wind fets : and it feems
almoft as if the fun had never fhone on the
ground, fince the creation. About fun fet
it cleared up, and we encamped on the laft
branch of *Sufquehanah*, the night following it
thundred and rained very faft, and took us

at

at a difadvantage, for we had made no fhelter to keep off the rain, neither could we fee it till juft over our heads, and it began to fall.

One of our *Indians* cut 4 fticks 5 feet long, and ftuck both ends into the ground, at 2 foot diftance, one from another; over thefe he fpread his match coat and crept through them, and then fell to finging: in the mean time we were fetting poles flantwife in the ground, tying others crofs them, over which we fpread our blanket and crept clofe under it with a fire before us and fell faft afleep.

I waked a little after midnight, and found our fire almoft out, fo I got the hatchet and felled a few faplings which I laid on, and made a roufing fire, tho' it rained ftoutly, and laying down once more, I flept found all night.

21*ft*, In the morning when we had dry'd our blankets, we kept along the fide of a hill, gradually afcending, the foil good, timber tall, and abundance of ginfeng; here the muf-quetoes were very troublefome, it being foggy, thence proceeding down a long gradual defcent on good rich foil with tall timber, fugar, ma-ple, chefnut, cherry, linden and elm, we tra-verfed a large valley and rivulet, then rode up a little fteep hill where we ftopped at half an hour after eleven, this hill was a little fandy, with fome large pines growing upon it; here we walked and looked about us, having not had fuch an opportunity for two days, during which

which time we had a fine prospect over the
vale of the great mountain we had just crossed,
and which differed so remarkably from all I
had ever been upon before, in its easy and fruitful ascent and descent, in its great width,
every where crowned with noble and lofty
woods, but above all, in its being intirely free
from naked rocks and steep precipices.

From these remarks, one might be naturally
led to imagine, that the Waters at the flood
gradually ebbed and retired on each side, towards the river *St. Lawrence* and *Susquehanah*,
the very next ridges on either side being nar-
rower, steeper, and some rocks washed bare,
and so all the adjacent ridges the farther they
are from this, appear to be more washed, more
composed of great banks of craggy rocks and
tremendous precipices, the soil more carried off,
mighty rocks tumbled down, and those left ap-
pearing as if piled up in a pyramid and hereby
preserved from a share in the awful ruin below
among their fellows; the soil being so perfectly washed from their root, as evidently no
longer to support them. After having enjoyed
this enchanting prospect and entertaining hypo-
thesis, we descended easily for several miles,
over good land producing sugar-maples, many
of which the *Indians* had tapped to make
sugar of the sap, also oaks, hickery, white
walnuts, plums and some apple trees, full of
fruit; the *Indians* had set long bushes all round
the

the trees at a little diftance, I fuppofe to keep
the fmall children from ftealing the fruit before
they were ripe: here we halted and turned our
horfes to grafs, while the inhabitants cleared a
cabin for our reception; they brought us
victuals, and we difpatched a meffenger immediately to *Onondago* to let them know
how near we were, it being within 4 miles.
All the *Indians*, men, women and children
came to gaze at us and our horfes, the little
boys and girls climbed on the roofs of their
cabins, about ten in number to enjoy a fuller
view, we fet out about ten, and travelled over
good land all the way, moftly an eafy defcent,
fome lime-ftone, then down the eaft hill, over
ridges of lime-ftone rock, but generally a moderate defcent into the fine vale where this
capital (if I may fo call it) is fituated.

We alighted at the council houfe, where
the chiefs were already affembled to receive us, which they did with a grave chear-
ful complaifance, according to their cuftom;
they fhew'd us where to lay our baggage, and
repofe ourfelves during our ftay with them;
which was in the two end apartments of this
large houfe. The *Indians* that came with us,
were placed over againft us: this cabin is about
80 feet long, and 17 broad, the common
paffage 6 feet wide, and the apartments on
each fide 5 feet, raifed a foot above the paffage
by a long fapling hewed fquare, and fitted
with

with joifts that go from it to the back of the
houfe; on thefe joifts they lay large pieces of
bark, and on extraordinary occafions fpread
matts made of rufhes, this favour we had; on
thefe floors they fet or lye down every one as
he will, the apartments are divided from each
other by boards or bark, 6 or 7 foot long,
from the lower floor to the upper, on which
they put their lumber, when they have eaten
their homony, as they fet in each apartment
before the fire, they can put the bowel over
head, having not above 5 foot to reach; they
fet on the floor fometimes at each end, but
moftly at one: they have a fhed to put their
wood into in the winter, or in the fummer,
to fet to converfe or play, that has a door
to the fouth; all the fides and roof of the cabin
is made of bark, bound faft to poles fet in the
ground, and bent round on the top, or fet
aflatt, for the roof as we fet our rafters; over
each fire place they leave a hole to let out the
fmoak, which in rainy weather, they cover
with a piece of bark, and this they can eafily
reach with a pole to pufh it on one fide or
quite over the hole, after this model are moft
of their cabins built, figure annexed.

The fine vale of *Onondago* runs north and
fouth, a little inclining to the weft, and is
near a mile wide, where the town is fituated
and excellent foil, the river that divides this
charming vale, is 2, 3 or 4 foot deep, very

G   full

full of trees fallen acrofs, or drove on heaps
by the torrents. The town in its prefent ftate
is about 2 or 3 miles long, yet the fcattered
cabins on both fides the water, are not above
40 in number, many of them hold 2 families,
but all ftand fingle, and rarely above 4 or 5
near one another; fo that the whole town is a
ftrange mixture of cabins, interfperfed with great
patches of high grafs, bufhes and fhrubs, fome
of peafe, corn and fquafhes, lime-ftone bottom
compofed of foffils and fea fhells.

It feems however, to have been more con-
fiderable when it became a conqueft to the
arms of *Lewis* 14th, at which time it muft
have been more compact, for hiftory relates
it to have been ftockadoed. The *Count de
Frontenac* governor of *Canada*, at the head
of the moft numerous army the *French* ever
drew together in *N. America*, had the fatisfaction in 1696 of triumphing over the afhes of
Onondago, whofe inhabitants terrified with
what they had heard of bombs, and generally
unwilling to hazard a fet battle, had already
abandoned their houfes after fetting them afire.
whatever glory the grand monarque might
reap from this exploit, it is certain he gained no other advantage, as a longer ftay
muft have inevitably ftarved the army, fo its
precipitate retreat helped our *Indians* to an
opportunity of taking their revenge by cutting

of

of every ftragling canoe, in their return by
water to *Monreal*.

At night, foon after we were laid down to
fleep, and our fire almoft burnt out, we were
entertained by a comical fellow, difguifed in
as odd a drefs as *Indian* folly could invent;
he had on a clumfy vizard of wood colour'd
black, with a nofe 4 or 5 inches long, a grining
mouth fet awry, furnifhed with long teeth,
round the eyes circles of bright brafs, furrounded by a larger circle of white paint,
from his forehead hung long treffes of buffaloes
hair, and from the catch part of his head ropes
made of the plated husks of *Indian* corn; I
cannot recollect the whole of his drefs, but
that it was equally uncouth: he carried in one
hand a large ftaff, in the other a calabafh with
fmall ftones in it, for a rattle, and this he
rubbed up and down his ftaff; he would
fometimes hold up his head and make a hide-
ous noife like the braying of an afs; he came
in at the further end, and made this noife at
firft, whether it was becaufe he would not
furprife us too fuddenly I can't fay: I ask'd
Conrad Weifer, who as well as myfelf lay
next the alley, what noife that was? and *Shickalamy* the *Indian* chief, our companion, who
I fuppofed, thought me fomewhat fcared,
called out, lye ftill *John*, I never heard him
fpeak fo much plain *Englifh* before. The jack-
pudding prefently came up to us, and an *Indian*

boy

boy came with him and kindled our fire, that
we might fee his glittering eyes and antick
poftures as he hobbled round the fire, fometimes
he would turn the Buffaloes hair on one fide
that we might take the better view of his ill-
favoured phyz, when he had tired himfelf,
which was fometime after he had well tired us,
the boy that attended him ftruck 2 or 3 fmart
blows on the floor, at which the hobgoblin
feemed furprifed and on repeating them he
jumped fairly out of doors and difappeared.
I fuppofe this was to divert us and get fome
tobacco for himfelf, for as he danced about
he would hold out his hand to any he came
by to receive this gratification which as often
as any one gave him he would return an awk-
ard compliment. By this I found it no new
diverfion to any but my felf. In my whim
I faw a vizard of this kind hang by the fide
of one of their cabins to another town. After this farce we endeavoured to compofe ourfelves to fleep but towards morning was again
difturbed by a drunken *Squaw* coming into
the cabin frequently complimenting us and
finging.

22*d.* was a fhowery day, and we ftirred
little out.

23*d.* we hired a guide to go with us to the
falt fpring, 4 or 5 miles off, down the river,
on the weft fide of it's mouth; being moft of
the way good land, and near the mouth very
rich:

rich: from whence it runs weftward near a quarter of a mile, a kind of a fandy beach adjoining to the bank of the river, containing 3 or 4 acres. Here the *Indians* dig holes, about 2 foot deep, which foon filling with brine, they dip their kettles, and boil the contents, until the falt remains at bottom; there was a family refiding at this time. The boys in the lake fifhing, the *Squaw* fetching water, gathering wood, and making a fire under the kettle, while the husband was basking himfelf on the fand, under the bufhes. We filled our gallon keg full of water and brought it to Town, where we boiled it to about a pound of falt. Our guides took their arrows, made of reed and down to fhoot fmall birds. About half way there is an excellent fpring of water, and by it a grove of *Curboroitæ* joining to a green fwamp, producing very high grafs. About a mile up the river from the lake, it runs by a fteep bank at the end of a high hill. The bank was fandy, and out of it run'd a brackifh water, which inclines me to think that there is a body of foffil falt here abouts, by which the plain is furnifhed with its intenfe falt brine, and that it is the vapour thereof that congeal to the trafh and bufhes that lye on the bank, and glitters like flakes of Ice, or Snow, in a Sunfhiny day. This day 2 deputies arrived from the *Cayugas* Country.

24*th*,

24th. *Lewis* and I hired a guide to go with us to *Oswego* for 16*s.* our intention was more to get provisions for our journey home, than to gratify our curiosity. In the mean time, *Conrad* stayed at *Onondago,* to treat with the *Indian* chiefs about the skirmish in *Virginia*; with a view to incline them singly in favour of our application, before they assembled in council: and here I cannot help observing, it was scarcely ever known, that an *Indian Chief* or *Councellor,* once gained so far as to promise him interest, did break his promise, whatever presents have been offered him from another quarter.

We travelled on foot to the *Onondago* lake, whence we had fetched the salt water the day before, there we procured a bark canoe at half an hour after eleven, then paddled down the lake, and reached the lower end in two hours course, N. W. This lake the *French* call *Ganentaha*; hence we went down the river a mile N. big enough to carry a large boat, if the trees fallen into it where but carried away, this brought us to the river from the *Cayuga* country, near 100 yards wide, very still, and so deep we could see no bottom, the land on both sides very rich and low to within a mile of the *Oneido* river, where the river began to run swift, and the bottom became visible, tho' at a good depth. At three o'clock we came to the last mention'd river, down which the *Abbany* trader come to *Oscuego,* half

a mile

a mile farther we came to a rippling, which
carried us with prodigious fwiftnefs down the
ftream, foon after we encountered a fecond,
and a mile farther a third, very rough. In
about an hour by the fun, after many other
ripplings, we found our felves at the great fall,
the whole breadth of the river which is above
100 yards wide and is eight or ten feet perpendicular: here we hawled our canoe afhore,
took out all our baggage, and carried it on our
back a mile to a little town, of about four or
five cabins; they chiefly fubfift by catching
fifh and affifting the *Alcany* people to haw'l
their *Bateans*, and carry their goods round the
falls; which may be about ten or twelve poles,
then they launch again into the river, and
down the foaming ftream that furioufly on all
fides dafhes one half againft the rocks, near a
mile before they come to ftill water, and indeed, it runs pretty fwift all the way to *Ofwego*. Thefe *Indians* were very kind to us,
and gave us boiled corn and water melons,
while they and our guide who was a relation
fat over againft us in the fame cabin, chewing
raw *Indian* corn ftalks, fpitting out the fub-
ftance after they fucked out the juice. But
we could not yet underftand whether we were
to go to the fort by land, or by water. In
the morning they had catched fome ftout eels,
and a great fifh two feet long, it was round
and thick, they ftrike them with long flender
fhafts

shafts 18 or 20 feet long, pointed at the end with iron see the shape. The 2 splints of wood spreading each side, directs the point into the fish, which at a great depth it would be otherwise difficult to hit. I saw upon one of their canoes in the morning a large piece of bark spread a-cross. On this lay gravel and sand, and on these coals and ashes, which I supposed had been a fire, and the gravel placed there to save the bark. And I took it to be a design both to allure and see to strike the fish.

25*th*. Our guide, and several other *Indians*, lead us to the canoes belonging to the town, into one of which we got full of hopes of going by water, but were much chagrin'd to find ourselves only paddled cross the water, where we unwillingly took out our cloaths, victuals and blankets, and carried them on our backs following our guides, who were now increased to three. We had 12 miles down the river by land, most of the way middling land, some white pine and spruce groves to pass through, but most of the way in sight of the river, which is very rapid most of the way to the lake. On the point formed by the entrance of the river, stands the fort or trading castle, it is a strong stone house, incompassed with a stone wall near 20 feet high, and 120 paces round, built of large squared stones; very curious for their softness, I cut my name in it with my knife. The town consists of about

70 log-

70 loghoufes, of which one half are in a row near the river, the other half oppofite to them, on the other fide of a fair were two ftreets divided by a row of pofts in the midft. Where each *Indian* has his houfe to lay his goods, and where any of the traders may traffick with him. This is furely an excellent regulation for preventing the traders from impofing on the *Indians*, a practife they have been formerly too much guilty of, and which has frequently involved the *Englifh* colonies in difficulties, and conftantly tended to depreciate us in the efteem of the natives; Who can fcarcely be blamed for judging of a nation, by the behaviour of thofe with whom they have the moft intercourfe. a judgment I am forry to confefs that has (till lately) tended much to the making them in favour rather of the French, than Englifh. I fpeak of private perfons, not of the refpective government. The chief officer in command at the caftle, keeps a good look out to fee when the *Indians* come down the lake with their poultry and furrs, and fends a canoe to meet them, which conducts them to the caftle, to prevent any perfon inticing them to put afhore privately, treating them with fpirituous liquors, and then taking that opportunity of cheating them. This officer feems very carefull, that all quarreling, and even the leaft mifunderftanding, when any happens, be quickly made up in an amicable manner, fince a fpeedy

H

accom-

accomodation can only prevent our country
men from incuring the imputation of injuſtice,
and the delay of it would produce the diſagree-
able conſequences of an *Indians* endeavouring
to right himſelf by force.

Oſwego, is an infant ſettlement made by the
province of *New-York*, with the noble view
of gaining to the crown of *Great Britain* the
command of the 5 lakes, and the dependence
of the *Indians* in their neighbourhood, and to
its ſubjects the benefit of the trade upon them,
and of the rivers that empty themſelves into
them. At preſent the whole navigation is carried
on by the *Indians* themſelves in bark canoes,
and there are perhaps many reaſons for deſiring
it ſhould continue ſo for ſome years at leaſt ;
but a good engliſhman cannot be without
hopes of ſeeing theſe great lakes become one
day accuſtomed to *Engliſh* navigation. It is
true, the famous fall of *Niagara*, is an inſur-
mountable bar to all paſſage by water, from
the lake *Ontario*, into the lake *Erie*, in ſuch
veſſels as are proper for the ſecure navigation
of either ; but beſides, that bark canoes are
carried on mens ſhoulders with eaſe, from one
to the other, as far as the paſſage is impracti-
cable : It will be much more eaſy to carry the
goods in waggons, from the upper lake,
into the *Huron* or *Quatoghie* lake, the ſtrait
is rendered unnavigable by the *Saute St. Marie*,
but a veſſel of conſiderable burthen may ſail

from

from the hither end of the *Erie* lake, to the
bottom of the lake *Michigan,* and for ought
we know, through all parts of the 3 middle
lakes. These lakes receive the waters of many
rivers, that in some places approach so near the
branches of the vast river *Mississippi,* that a
short land carriage supplies the communication.
And here to use the words of a most judicious
writer, " He that reflects on the natural state
" of that continent must open to himself a
" a field for traffick in the southern parts of *N.*
" *America,* and by the means of this river
" and the lakes, the imagination takes into
" view such a scene of inland navigation; as
" cannot be paralleled in any other part of
" the world.

The honour of first discovering these extensive fresh water seas, is certainly due to the
French, who are at this time in possession of
settlements at *Fort Ponchartrian,* on the strait
between *Lake Erie* and the *Lake Huron* and
at *Misilimahinac* between the latter and the
upper lake, but as these can give them no title against the original inhabitants or the *five
nations,* Conquerors of all the adjacent nations, so it is difficult to conceive by what ar-
guments these small posts, inhabited by no sub-
jects of *France* but soldiers, can be extended to
mark any possession beyond the reach of
their gun's, or land actually cultivated, ex-
cept by such as must intitle the crown of *Great*

H 2   *Britain*

Britain to all *North America*, both as *prior discoverers* and prior planters, without a subsequent desertion.

The traders from *New York* come hither, up the *Mohawks* river, which discharges itself into *Hudsons* river, but generally go by land from *Albany*, to *Schenectady* about 20 miles from the *Mohawks* river, the carriage is but 3 miles into the river that falls into the *O-neido* lake, which discharges itself by the *Oneida* river, into the *Onondago* river, and brings their goods to *Oswego* in the manner I have before related.

We came to the town about 12 o'clock, the commissary invited us to the castle where we dined, together with the Doctor and Clerk. After dinner we had the satisfaction of swimming in the lake *Ontario*, which is some times called by our *Indians Cadarakin*, this is also the name of a french fort upon it, almost opposite to *Oswego*, N. it has 4 bastions built of stone, and is near half a mile in circumference; it stands where the waters of this lake are already formed into the river St. Lawrence, which makes a good road for great barks under the point of *Cadarakin Bay*. The famous and unfortunate Mr. *De la Sale* had two barks which remains sunk there to this day.

These lakes are said to have a kind of flux and reflux peculiar, since it is affirmed to be sensibly ebb and flood several times in a quarter of an hour, tho' it be perfectly smooth and

scarce

ſcarce any wind. But it is evident from the face of the earth, that the water of the lake *Ontario* is conſiderably diminiſhed and has loſt ground a great number of years, for the ſhores above a mile within land, are abundantly more low, as well as of a looſer texture then the ſoil beyond, whether this effect is in common to all the waters on the earth, according to a conjecture of the great Sir *Iſaac Newton :* Or whether it be not at (leaſt in part) owing to the removal of ſome great obſtruction, which by cauſing a fall in the river St. *Lawrence,* might formerly pen the waters up to a greater height than now ; or only to the gradual wearing away by the perpetual paſſage of the water over thoſe falls that ſtill ſubſiſt *:* or to a caſual ruin of ſome part of one of them, I ſhall leave to the determination of a more able naturaliſt than myſelf.

The water was very clear and as cold as our river in May, it is well taſted and ſuppoſed to be 120 miles broad, and near 200 long, ſtreaching N. N. W. but this muſt be an error, the common maps giving it a bearing to the Northward of the lake, but Mr. *Bellin* ſhews us it lies E. and W. from the obſervations of *P.Charlevoix,* on the exactneſs of which he thinks he cannot too much relie, and *Bellin* in his map of theſe lakes has given it this
bearing

bearing. We lodged in the castle in the captains chamber.

26th. Early in the morning I walked out looking for plants, as I had done the evening before. I observed a kitchen garden and a grave yard to the S. W. of the castle; which puts me in mind that the neighbourhood of this lake is esteemed unhealthful, we were entertained by one of the traders, with whom we breakfasted; and bought of him some dryed beef. And a gallon of Rum we got at the castle. The traders had disposed of most of their biscuit and had packed up their provision, in order to return directly to *Albany* : however, one of them went about to the rest and collected us a good parcel of biscuit, a kindness we were very sensible of. After breakfast I regulated my journal, having a convenient private room to do it in. We dined at the castle, and at 3 o'clock set out for *Onondago*. Two *Indians* helped to carry some of our baggage; the day was warm, the *Indians* walked fast our load was heavy and we were sufficiently weary before we reached the town near the falls, which was about sun set. Indeed we had the favour of shady woods all the way, we lodged where we did before. The *Indian Squaws* got very drunk and made a sad noise till morning. My fear least our guide was drunk also, added a good deal to an indisposition I was seiz'd with in the evening,

but

but in the morning I found him and his companion, to my great joy, faft afleep by the outfide of the cabin.

27th, We fet out early and found our canoe fafe where we left it, and it was with much fatisfaction that I entered it. At half an hour after ten, we got to the firft fall, above the great one, the *Indians* brought the canoe to fhore and made fign for us to difembark and walk along afhore, while they ftept into the river, and hawled the canoe up the fall about a quarter of a mile, by good land. We reimbarked again, and at twelve came to the *Oneido* branch, up which the *Albany* traders return, after 2 or 3 months trade at *Ofwego-Caftle*. At 3 o'clock we entered the *Onondago* lake, the upper end of which we gained by five, the land about the lake is pretty good and fome large marfhes and rich low ground moftly on each fide, but here and there the hills come clofe to the water: I think it muft be eight miles long and above one broad, very brackifh at the falt plain; very deep in fome places near the middle, but fhallow for 100 yards from the fhore. The *Indians* paddled the canoe a little way higher up the ftream and might have brought us to the town, if the fallen trees had been removed; but whatever nature has done for them (and fhe is no where more bountiful) they are too lazy by any trouble of their own to improve; but when compelled by the moft urgent neceffity.　　We

We reached the town about sun-set, equally pleased with our having improved the opportunity so well by seeing *Ontario* lake, and that we were returned safe to the interpreter and *Indian Chiefs*; those two last days had been pretty warm : our *Indian* guide was a sullen, illnatured, and I believe, a superstitious fellow. Every now and then as we paddled up the river, he would with a composed countenance utter somewhat pretty loud for about the space of two minutes at a time, whether it was a magical incantation, or a prayer, I can't tell; I am satisfied it was no song, nor any speech directed to us, or the *Indian* with him, for he seemed intirely unmoved all the time.

28*th*, This was a rainy thundering warm day, and two deputies arrived from the *Oneidoes*. News came that the worms had destroyed abundance of corn and grass in *Canada*. This night we were troubled with fleas, and what was worse, our men exceeding drunk and noisy ; our grievances in the day were more tolerable, being only women infesting us with their company and bawling, in great good humour, indeed I perceived to no quarrel while among them.

29*th*, Several more deputies arrived from the *Tuscaroroes*, we went to visit a poor emaciated *Indian*, who they said was bewitched, he lived about a mile from the *Council-House*.

This

This day was warm, and several showers passed by to the southward.

30th, Three of the *Mohawks* arrived, this nation dwells farthest within the province of *New-York*, and to the southward of the river known by their name; abundance of whites live among them, and as they are the best acquainted with the manners of the *English*, so they have at all times shewn the most steady affection to our people. I am sorry to say, their morals are little if at all mended by their frequent intercourse with us Christians, tho' I am persuaded it is not the fault of our religion but its professors, perhaps this may be esteemed a principal cause why they are become less numerous than any of their confederates.

This morning after breakfast, I went to the east hill, and found a fine spring on the west side, surrounded with *Arbor Vitæ*, some a foot diameter, this water is of such a petrifying nature, that as it runs among the fallen leaves it incrusts them and petrifies in great stones as big as one can well lift; there was a great piece of ground covered with them, which had turned the water-course several times, I have seen three of these springs in my travels; one on the other side of *Potomack* and one up *Delawars* at *Menesinks*; this hill is good limestone land, producing sugar maple, elms, beech, and some white pine, which

last

laſt had then 3 or 4 cones, on 2 or 3 trees, but they were quite green.

This afternoon the chiefs met in council, and three of them ſpoke for near a quarter of an hour each, two of theſe while ſpeaking, walked backward and forward in the common paſſage, near 2 thirds of its length, with a ſlow even pace, and much compoſure and gravity in their countenance; the other delivered what he had to ſay ſitting in the middle, in a graceful tone exhorting them to a cloſe indiſſoluble amity and unanimity, for it was by this perfect union their forefathers had conquered their enemies, were reſpected by their allies, and honoured by all the world; that they were now met according to their antient cuſtom, tho' ſeveral imminent dangers ſtood in their way, mountains, rivers, ſnakes and evil ſpirits, but that by the aſſiſtance of the *great Spirit* they now ſaw each others faces according to appointment.

This the interpreter told me was the opening of the diet, and was in the opinion of theſe people abundantly ſufficient for one day, ſince there is nothing they contemn ſo much as precipitation in publick councils; indeed they eſteem it at all times a mark of much levity in any one to return an immediate anſwer to a ſerious queſtion however obvious, and they conſequently ſpin out a Treaty, where many points are to be moved, to a great length of

time,

time, as is evident from what our conference
with them, produced afterward at *Lancaster*
begun the 22d of *June* 1744.

This council was followed by a feaft, after
4 o'clock we all dined together upon 4 great
kettles of *Indian* corn foop, which we foon
emptied, and then every chief retired to his
home.

31*ft*, In the morning, as foon as light, I
walked out to look at our horfes as ufual,
and clofe by a cabin fpied a knife almoft
covered with grafs; I fuppofed it loft, but
the *Indians* being not yet ftiring let it lie:
a little after fun-rife I walked there again,
and the *Squaw* being at the door, fhewed
her where it lay, at which fhe feemed exceeding pleafed, and picked it up immediately.
As I came back to our cabin, I fpy'd 2 *Indian*
girls at play with beans, which they threw
from one to the other on a match coat fpread
between them; as they were behind our cabin, I turned to fee how they play'd, but
they feemed much out of countenance, and
run off in an inftant: I obferved that the *Indian* women are generally very modeft.

About noon the council fat a 2*d* time, and
our interpreter had his audience, being charge
by the governor with the conduct of the treaty.
Conrad Weifar had engaged the *Indian* fpeaker
to open the affair to the chiefs affembled in
council; he made a fpeech near half an hour,

and delived 3 broad belts and 5 ftrings of *Wampum* to the council, on the proper occa-fions. There was a pole laid a-crofs from one chamber to another over the paffage, on this their belts and ftrings were hung, that all the council might fee them, and here have the matters in remembrance, in confirma-tion of which they were delivered : The con-ference held till 3, after which we dined , this repaft confifted of 2 great kettles of *Indian* corn foop, or thin homony, with dry'd eels and other fifh boiled in it, and one kettle full of young fquafhes and their flowers boiled in water, and a little meal mixed ; this difh was but weak food, laft of all was ferved a great bowl, full of *Indian* dumplings, made of new foft corn, cut or fcraped off the ear, then with the addition of fome boiled beans, lapped well up in *Indian* corn leaves, this is good hearty provifion. After dinner, we had a favourable anfwer, coroborated by feveral belts of *Wampum*, with a fhort fpeech to each, thefe we carried away as our tokens of peace and friendfhip, the harangue concluded with a charge to fit ftill as yet, for tho' they had difpatched our bufinefs firft, it was not be-caufe they were weary of us, but to make us eafy. This complement preceded other bufinefs, which lafted till near fun fet, when we regaled on a great bowl of boiled cakes, 6 or 7 inches diameter, and about 2

thick,

thick, with another of boiled fquafh; foon after, the chiefs in a friendly manner took their leave of us, and departed every one to his lodging: this night we treated two of the chiefs that lived in the council hall, which as I mentioned, was our quarters; they drank chearfully, wifhing a long continuance of uninterrupted amity between the *Indians* and *Englifh*.

Auguft 1. Six of the *Anticoque Indians* had an audience, but when they came to it, could not make themfelves underftood, tho' provided with an interpreter brought near 700 miles, (they faid more) but he could not underftand the *Mohawk* Language, but only the *Delawar* and middling *Englifh*, * fo they contrived he fhould direct his fpeech to *Conrad Weifar* in *Englifh*, and interpret this to the council. They gave broad belts of *Wampum*, 3 arm belts and 5 ftrings; one was to wipe clean all the blood they had fpilt of the *five nations*, another to raife a tumulus over their graves, and to pick

---

* *P. Charlevoix*, perhaps from his own knowledge and the information he has received from his brother miffionaries, tells us, that the languages of the northern part of *North America*, are properly 3, the *Sioux* or *Nadouiffiour*, called by the *Englifh Norway*, the *Algonquin* or *Adirondack*, and the *Huron* or *Quatoghie* of which laft he makes the *Iroquois* called by our author the *Mohawk*, a dialect; but adds, he knew not what language is talked by the *Cherokees*, whether the language of the *Antecoques* be a dialect of the laft which is very poffible, or of the *Adirondack* which I take the *Delawar* to be, I can't determine.

pick out the sticks, roots or stones, and make it smooth on the top, a third, to cleanse the stomach of the living from gall or any thing else that made them sick; a fourth was a cordial to chear up their spirits; a fifth, to cloath their bodies and keep them warm, a sixth, to join them in mutual friendship, a seventh, to request them to let them settle on a branch of *Susqehanah*, another to intreat the 5 nations that they would take a little care to protect their women from insults while out a hunting, and the rest for such like purposes. This business lasted 4 hours, then we dined on *Indian* corn and squash soop, and boiled bread. In the afternoon, I went on the western mountain as I had the day before on the eastern; it was very rich and full of tall timber quite to the top, the trees were linden, elm, sugar-maple, white walnut, oak, hickery and chesnut, besides ginseng, and most sort of herbs that grow on our rich lime-stone land.

These 2 days the wind was south and warm and several showers to the S. E. The council met-at 9 o'clock, and the kettles of soop and a basket of dumplings were brought in for our dinner; after dinner the *Anticoques* delivered a belt and a string of *Wampum*, with a complaint that the *Marylanders* had deposed their king, and desired leave to chuse one for themselves: to this, as well as all the articles opened yesterday, the chiefs returned plausible

but

but fubtil anfwers; then they gave us 2 ftrings withal, telling us, that now they had thrown water on our fire, and we were at liberty to return home when we pleafed, they all took their leave, and bid us adieu by fhaking hands very kindly, and feemingly with much affection. This night the young men getting into liquor, kept fhouting and finging till morning.

3*d*, We prepared for fetting forward, and many of the chiefs came once more to take their farewell; fome of them brought us provifion for our journey, we fhook hands again and fet out at 9.

It was greatly to my mortification, that I was forced to return for the moft part the fame way I came. We had intended to go through the *Mohawks* country to *Albany*, but our 2 *Indians* could not be perfuaded to go that way, tho' we offered to bear their charges, and the chiefs were not willing we fhould leave them to pafs through the wildernefs alone, as they came to gratify us and further our bufinefs. This day was fair, and the wind S. In the afternoon, we afcended that lovely mountain S. W. which divides the waters that render tribute to the great ftreams of *St. Laurence* and *Sufquehanah*. We did not directly crofs the mountain, but rode a fmall way on its fummit under the grateful fhade of thofe lofty trees that every way adorn it, and
after-

afterwards we traveled feveral miles on its S. W. fide, where we enjoyed a fine profpect of a fpacious rich vale on our left hand. On this hill we faw a lime ftone a little bigger than my head, which is rare in thefe parts.

We entered the vale at 5, then croffed a *run* and rode along a rich level for feveral miles, and under the delightful protection of very tall trees that brought us to a creek, a branch of *Sufquehanah*, where we lodged furrounded by ginfeng

4*th*, This was a fine day, and our traveling cool, becaufe fhady, and the goosberries being now ripened, we were every now and then tempted to break off a bough and divert ourfelves with picking them, tho' on horfeback.

5*th*, This morning was clear and cool, and now our journey was truly charming, it is fcarce poffible to think the advantage we had in returning from the fingle circumftance of being free from thofe fmall gnats that tormented us in our going fo grievoufly. But our return being moftly in the fame path, it will be needlefs to defcribe the land or its productions again.

6*th*, We fet out an hour before funrife, the morning clear, at half an hour after ten we reached *Owagan*, and turned our horfes to grafs, while we ftopped at a cabin. The *Squaw* brought in a bowl of huckle-berries,

to

to ſtay our ſtomachs, and ſoon after a large
kettle full of ſmall homony boil'd in ſtrong
veniſon broth; this was noble entertainment,
and too good to leave any of. I heartily
pityed the poor *Squaw*, for I believe ſhe had
dreſſed it for herſelf and ſeveral children : ſhe
alſo obliged us to accept of a fine piece of
veniſon to carry away. Here we killed a rattle ſnake, the ſecond we had ſeen to day : at
one we continued our journey through groves of
pine of a ſtupendous ſtature; the land midling for 2 miles S. W. to the river, then a
variable courſe over land of equal goodneſs,
oak and hickery, ſome bottoms rich; and by
three we croſs'd a fine creek where we ſpyed
a grey ſquirrel which our *Indian* would have
ſhot, had it not been on the top of a white
oak : here we found very ſtony ground, great
ſtones having been drove by one common
force, into a form like that of fiſh ſcales,
yet this was a mile from the river, and many
yards perpendicular above the bed of it, this
may be the effects of the univerſal deluge, or
ſome mighty torrent of water ſince that, muſt
have flowed over theſe ſtones and waſhed them
thus bare. We travelled till about two hours
by the ſun, and then pitched by the river,
which run full W. there was high barren
mountains on the upper ſide, here the river
was deep and ſmooth enough for flat bottom'd
veſſels, which made us heartily wiſh that we

K   were

were in a canoe, and our horfes at *Shamokin*, for we dreaded the difmal wildernefs between. We obferved here an old log, which the bears had cunningly turned to pick up the fnails, beetles, and grubbs, that had crept under it for fhelter.

7th, We rod over middling land, producing oak, pine, and great magnolia, to the *Tohicon* town on the *Cayugo* branch; this place we ar- rived at by noon but ftayed there all night, frighted by feveral fhowers that paffed over the mountains in fight: indeed it rained a little here, I walked to the branch after dinner, and found abundance of foffils on the banks, but the diftance of the way, and heavy load of our baggage, were an infurmountable bar to my bringing any home. This day the *Anticoque* interpreter that travelled with us from *Onondago*, who left the path a little to hunt, misd our tract and hit upon an *Indian* town, 3 miles up the branch, and there picking up a *Squaw* brought her with him. The chief man of the town came to vifit us in a very friendly manner, and our interpreter telling him where we had been, what about, and how well we had fucceeded; he teftified abundance of fatisfaction that peace was not like to be interrupted, he added, when he came home his people told him, we had paffed through their town, but that we had not informed them of our bufinefs.

This

This furnishes us with an instance of the
Punctilio the *Indians* constantly treat travellers
with, the people though earnestly desiring to
know our commission, would not - take the
liberty to ask us. This night our fellow
traveller lodged with his occasional wife in a
corner of our cabin, and in the morning
would have taken her with him at our ex-
pence, to the great vexation of Mr *Weisar*, who
thought it intolerable that an intruder should
gratifie his private inclinations to the short-
ning of our necessary provisions, already in-
sufficient; as we did not take much pains to
conceal this resentment, he had determined to
part with her, though with much regret, and
accordingly left her when we crossed the
branch, giving her a farewell shout; we
heard this with much joy, and I believe it
was as well for the parties.

8*th*,We continued our journey without meet-
ing any thing worth remarking, the ground we
had passed rode over in our way out, and had
lodged at the very creek we spent this night at.

9*th*. We travelled to a fine creek big enough
to drive two mills, we stoped for this night at
the foot of a great hill, cloathed with large
Magnolia, 2 feet diameter and 100 feet high;
perfectly straight, shagbark-hickery, chesnut
and chesnut oak. This is like a bridge between the N.E. and N.W. branches of *Sufquehanah*: here is also a spring from whence
the water runs to both branches.

10*th*,

10th *August*, We set out, the sun half an
our high, travelled along a rich hill side, where
we observ'd a pretty many rocks, then down to a
Licking-place by 8, where our intruder who was
a good way before us shot at an Elk, and having
wounded him, pursued him several hours. We
waited his return till 2 o'clock, *Lewis Evans*
took an observation here, and found the lat.
41. a half. Set out again at 3, and travelled
over fine rich ground by a creek where we
lodged. I took a fancy to ascend 2 thirds of
the height of a neighbouring hill, in the way I
came to abundance of loose stones, and very craggy rocks, which seemed to threaten impending
ruin, the soil was black and very rich, full
of great wild stinging nettles, as far as I went
I rolled down several loose stones to make a
path for my more expeditious return. This
I found the *Indians* much disturbed at, for
they said it would infallibly produce rain the
next day, I told them I had sufficient experience, it signified nothing, for it was my common practice to roll down stones from the top
of every steep hill, and could not recollect that
it ever rained the next day, and that I was almost sure to morrow would be a very fair day.

11th, We got out before sun rise, and rode
over very good bottoms of *Linden*, *Poplar* and
Elm, we killed a rattle snake, and soon after
found a patch of *Chamerododendron*, at 8 we
came to a creek winding from between the
mountains

mountains on the left, then along a level to
another from the right, which we croſſed to
our former cabin. Quickly after we reached
a bad hill, where I firſt found the *Ginſeng* in
th s journey, the ſoil was black and light, with
flat ſtones facing the eaſt, there we paſſed by
9, then over a bottom of laurel and pine to a
creek we had ſeveral times croſſed, when ob-
ſtructed as frequently we were by hills, keep
ing cloſe to the water on the ſide we were riding.   At 10 we left this creek for the ſake
o a ſhorter way than we came, for this pur-
poſe we kept a S. courſe to the top of a high
but very poor hill, which we reached about a qr.
after eleven, and had a proſpect ſtill to a gap
we were to paſs to the river; the northſide of
this hill was cloathed with tall ſpruce, while
pine and beech, the top with cheſnut, ſcrubby
oak and huckle berries, the S. ſide with ſhrub,
honeyſuckles &c.   Our way was now over a
poor pebble ſtoney vale of laurel, ſpruce firr,
pine, cheſnut, and huckle berries, to a *Run* of
water; where we dined on parched meal
mixed with water. We left that place at half
an hour after one, and ſoon found ourſelves
much diſtreſſed by the broad flat ſtones on the
ſide of the hill, our way lay over. Our horſes.
could hardly ſtand, but even ſlipt on their ſides
on our left a rivulet ruſhed from a precipice,
and the mountains were ſo ſteep and cloſe to
its ſides, that we were oblidged to climb to the
top

top of that on the weſt; here we ſuffered our horſes to reſt while we gathered huckle berries to eat, we travelled on the top a good way all ſtony to the point, which was very narrow, and the flat ſtones on each ſide turned up like the ridge of a houſe, this reminded me of *Dr. Burnets Theory*, and his ingenious *Hypotheſis*, to account for the formation of mountains. The deſcent was moderate, the land middling, oak, cheſnut and huckle-berries: we found a *Run* here and repoſed ourſelves for this night, having ſupped on veniſon, ſhot by our *Indians* who left us on the hill that evening. It was fair and plea-ſant, and the great green graſs-hopper began to ſing (*Catedidiſt*) theſe were the firſt I ob-ſerved this year. Before day break it began to rain, it laſted about an hour and then ceaſ-ed. The *Indians* inſiſted that was cauſed by the ſtones I rolled down 2 days ago, I told the *Antecoque Indians* if their obſervations had any truth it ſhould have been the day before, which was remarkably fair. To this he cuningly replyed, that our *Almanacks* often prognoſti-cated on a day, and yet the rain did not come within two days.

12th, This day, the land produced middling oak, pitch, pine, and huckleberries, ſometimes pebbles and a ſhallow ſoil. We dined on veniſon (partly our own, and partly given us by the *Indians*) at a deſerted town about 7 miles off: this is called the *French* town, from a *French* woman

woman who married a *Delawar Indian*, and conformed to their manners ; she left several children behind her, who were now come to look after their horses and break the young ones. It rained very fast for an hour, and in the midst of it about half a score of the 5 *Nations*, who had been on the back of *S. Carolina* to fight the *Catawba's*, passed very fast through the town with one poor female prisoner, they shouted couragiously, but we learnt no particulars of this great enterprize: about 3 it cleared up, we crossed the creek and travelled about 10 miles, most of the way good rich land, extensive bottoms and high grass : I saw one lovely white *Lychnus* 5 feet high. Near night it began to rain, and we made a bark cabin, which kept us pretty dry, the rain continued all night with thunder.

13*th*, It cleared up early in the morning. We moved forward to our first cabin, where we dined on parched meal, which is some of the best *Indians* travelling provision. We had of it 2 bags, each a gallon, from the *Indians* at *Onondago*, the preparation of it is thus. They take the corn and parch it in hot ashes, till it becomes brown, then clean it, pound it in a mortar and sift it; this powder is mixt with sugar. About 1 qr. of a pint, diluted in a pint of water, is a hearty traveling dinner, when 100 miles from any inhabitants : about 2 hours after seting out we came near the river. Here

5

5 of us rode over a great rattle fnake unfeen and unhurt. I perceived him juft as my mare was over him; a little further we faw another juft by us. We travelled till near fun fet, when 2 of our *Indians* were taken with a bad fit of an ague, this obliged us to encamp by the river, where our horfes had excellent food. At about 20 rods from it I faw a bank much higher up, being near 30 feet perpendicular above the furface of the water, raifed gradually to this height by the frequent floods, which this weftern branch is much fubject too. Thus by fand continually heaped upon the firm fand, it is become a ftrong fand bank.

14*th*, We paffed through an old town, where we found plumbs, peaches, and noble clufters of large grapes growing, very deep in fand, left about them by the flood I mentioned juft now; a little farther the land was rich and low, covered with high weeds and grafs, with locuft, linden, walnut and elm, the higher land with elm and oak. At 11 o'clock we reached *Shamokin*, here we boiled dumplins and had plenty of water melons; we ftayed all night.

15*th*, Next day by noon we came to *Moho-nyoy*, where we ftayed dinner, in the afternoon we rode over fome ftony poor land, then piney, white oak, and fome middling land.

16*th*, This morning I was entertained with the Mufical howling of a wolf, which I had

not

not heard for many years, but my companions were too faft afleep to hear it, we fet out early and by one had croffed the 3 ridges of the *blue mountains*, and the 2 fpruce vales, were the branches of *Swatara* ran, and dined in St. *Anthonys Wildernefs*, as *Count Zinzendorf* has named it. We mounted again at 2 and climbed up the S. ridge, and at the top let our horfes reft, for they were cover'd with fweat. In the mean time we look'd for water, but found none, in this fearch we found an *Indian Squaw* drying huckle berries. This is done by fetting 4 forked fticks, in the ground, about 3 or 4 feet high, then others a-crofs, over them the ftalks of our common *Jacea* or *Saratula*, on thefe lie the berries, as malt is fpread on the hair cloth over the kiln. Underneath fhe had kindled a fmoke fire, which one of her children was tending. The quantity of their huckle berries growing on and between thefe ridges, is prodigious, the top of the S. ridge is pretty good land, and affords a fine profpect of the great and fertile vale of *Tulpihocken*, the ridge itfelf is pleafant. When we had refted ourfelves and our poor tired horfes, we lead them moft of the way for 20 miles, this gave us an opportunity of gathering what quantity we pleafed of their berries, tho' we eat rather more than I thought we might fafely venture on, yet we found no ill confequence from our excefs. When we were defcended we had but

L   2 miles

2 miles to a houfe, where we lodged, it rained faft in the evening and great part of the night itfelf. And we heartily congratulated ourfelves on the enjoyment of good bread, butter and milk, in a comfortable houfe, and clean ftraw to fleep on, free from fleas.

17*th*, Though my mare was fo lame, fhe had not ftirred 20 yards all night, yet we got this day by noon to Mr *Conrad Weifars*; but under the difficulty of carrying my baggage good part of the way on my back, befides being fcarcely able to get her along: when fhe came into the pafture, fhe ftretched herfelf at full length and rofe no more for 24 hours. In the afternoon I fpent my time on Mr *Weifar's* high hill, gathering of feeds: here the great vale and blue mountains form a lovely profpect.

18*th*, I borrowed a horfe of Mr *Weifar*, and fet up all night at *Monatawony*.

19*th*, Before funfet, I had the pleafure of feeing my own houfe and family: I found them in good health, and with a fincere mind, I returned thanks to the almighty power, that had preferved us all.

In this journey into the heart of a country, ftill in the poffeffion of it's original inhabitants: I could not help fometimes to divert the length of the way by reflecting on their manners, their complection fo different from ours, and their Traditions: this led me to conjecture at their origin, or whence

whence they came into *America*, and at what
time. Perhaps it may be equally hard to dif-
prove or to prove that they were originally
placed here by the fame creator who made the
world, as foon as this part of it became ha-
bitable, for it is reafonable to fuppofe the
almighty power provided for the peopling
of this, as well as of the other fide of the
globe, by a fuitable ftock of the human
fpecies.

However if we are to account for their
paffing from what is called the old world,
there are many relations of voyages hither
from the North of *Europe*, previous to that of
Columbus, which though dark and uncertain,
are neither evidently fabulous, nor even im-
probable from either the length or difficulties
of the way. That the *Norwegians*, the pof-
feffors of *Iceland*, for many ages paft had
colonies in *Greenland*, is a fact too well
attefted to admit a doubt, from *Greenland*
the fhort paffage crofs *Daon's Streights* brings
us into the continent of *America*. If thefe
colonies be put out of the queftion, it is fcarce
poffible to think, that of the numerous fleets
with which the *Danes* and *Norwegians* terrified continually the reft of *Europe*, none
tempted by the hopes of gain, or drove by ftrefs
of weather, fhould ever fall in with the coafts
of *Newfoundland* or *Gulph of St. Lawrence*.
If it be objected that the navigators of thofe
times

times were too unskilfull to attempt such a discovery, does it not furnish us with a reason to account for its being made by chance. If this passage was ever publickly known, which is more probable it was not, might not the knowledge of it be lost as that to *Greenland*, and can we be sure that the *Greenland* of the *Norwegians* was not more to the southward of that country now so called. I am not ignorant that these traditions of the *Norwegian* colonies, as well as many others to the same point, particularly that of prince *Madoc* has been treated as meer fiction ; but let us not forget that *Herodotus's* account of the doubling the Cape of *Good Hope* has been treated so likewise too, tho' the fact be now established to the degree of moral certainty.

Again, it is not unlikely but there may be land most of the way from *America* to *Japan*, at least islands, separated only by narrow channels, and in sight, or nearly so, of one another. I have been lately informed of an *Indian* woman, well known by a person in *Canada*, and after an interval of many years met again by the same person in *Chinese Tartary* ; he could not be convinced she was the same, till by discourse he had with her, she told him, that being made captive by a neighbouring nation, she had during many years been transferred by captivity, sale, or gift, from one nation to another till she was brought where

he

he found her. If this be true it muſt be *Continent* moſt of the way.

Another manner of peopling this ſide of the earth, particularly *S. America*, might be by ſome veſſels of the *Egyptians*, *Phænicians*, or *Carthaginians* being blown off the coaſt of *Guinea* to that of *Brazil*, or the *Antilles* in their courſe, to or from the cape of *Good-Hope*; in which caſe, for want of thoſe *Arts* and *Sciences* which are not to be found in *America*, before it's plantation by the whites, and which are ſeldom to be met with in a ſhips crew, they muſt take to that way of life our *Indians* now follow. This conjecture is the more probable, as even in the ſtate of perfecti-on, the art of navigation is now arrived at, this accident is often unavoidable.

But whatever was their origin, our ſix nati-ons may be now thus characteriſed: they are a ſubtile, prudent, and judicious people in their councils, indefatigable, crafty, and re-vengeful in their wars, the men lazy and in-dolent at home, the women continual ſlaves, modeſt, very loving, and obedient to their husbands. As to the natural diſpoſition of theſe *Nations*, they are grave, ſolid, and ſtill in their recreations, as well as in their councils. The *Delawar's* and *Suſquehanah's*, on the contrary, are very noiſy in their recreations, and loud in diſcourſe; but all when in liquor, whether men or women, take the liberty of

ſhouting

shouting, singing, and dancing at an extravagant rate, till the operations of the liquor cease; or being wearied they fall asleep.

The six nations enjoy the character of being the most warlike people in *N. America*, this they have acquired by the uninterrupted state of war, they have continued in probably near 200 years, and which has been attended with such success, that has made them the dread of people above 1000 miles distant. It cannot however be supposed, but they have frequently met with several checks, especially since the *French* assisted all their enemies openly near these 100 years past.

Their wars were formerly carried on with much more cruelty then of late, their prisoners who had the misfortune to fall into their hands, being generally tortured to death, now their numbers being very much diminished by constant wars, with both distant and neighbouring nations, and perhaps a good deal partly by the spirituous liquors, and diseases the Europeans have brought among them. They very politically strive to strengthen themselves not only by alliances with their neighbours, but the prisoners they take; they are almost always accepted by the relations of a warrior slain in his place, and thus a boy of 15, is sometimes called father by men of 30. This naturalizes them of course, and unites them into the tribe the deceased belonged to. This

custom

cuſtom is as antient as our knowledge of them, but when their number of warriours was more than twice as many as now, the relations would more frequently refuſe to adopt the priſoner, but rather chuſe to gratify their thirſt of revenge.

Their religious notions are very confuſed and much mixed with ſuperſtition. Yet they ſeem not only to acknowledge a deity, but e-ven to worſhip him in unity and ſpirit. What benefits they receive, they aſcribe to a di-vine power. They have ſtrange notions of ſpirits, conjuration, and witchcraft : theſe are agreeable to their blindneſs, and want of proper education among them, for I have al-ways obſerved, that the belief of ſupernatu-ral powers in a meer man, generally prevails in proportion to a Perſon's ignorance.

A Letter from Mr. KALM, *a Gentleman of* Sweden, *now on his Travels in* America, *to his Friend in* Philadelphia ; *containing a particular Account of the* GREAT FALL *of* Niagara.

S I R, *Albany, Sep.* 2, 1750.

AFter a pretty long journey made in a ſhort time, I am come back to this town. You may remember, that when I took my leave of you, I told you, I would this ſummer, if time permitted, take a view of *Niagara* FALL,
esteemed

efteemed one of the greateſt curioſities in the World. When I came laſt year from *Quebec*, you enquir'd of me ſeveral particulars concerning this fall; and I told you what I heard of it in *Canada*, from ſeveral *French* gentlemen who had been there: but this was ſtill all hearſay ; I could not aſſure you of the truth of it, becauſe I had not then ſeen it myſelf, and ſo it could not ſatisfy my own, much leſs your curioſity. Now, ſince I have been on the ſpot, it is in my power to give you a more perfect and ſatisfactory deſcription of it.

After a fatiguing travel, firſt on horſeback thro' the country of the *Six Indian Nations*, to *Oſwego*, and from thence in a Canoe upon lake *Ontario*, I came on the 12th of *Auguſt* in the evening to *Niagara* fort. The *French* there ſeemed much perplexed at my firſt coming, imagining I was an *Engliſh* officer, who under pretext of ſeeing *Niagara* Falls, came with ſome other view; but as ſoon as I ſhew'd them my paſſports, they chang'd their behaviour, and received me with the greateſt civility. *Niagara* Fall is ſix *French* leagues from *Niagara* Fort. you firſt go three leagues by water up *Niagara* river, and then three leagues over the carrying place. As it was late when I arriv'd at the Fort, I could not the ſame day go to the Fall, but I prepar'd myſelf to do it the next morning. The commandant

of

of the Fort, Monſr. *Beaujon*, invited all the officers and gentlemen there to ſupper with him. I had read formerly almoſt all the authors that have wrote any thing about this Fall; and the laſt year in *Canada*, had made ſo many enquiries about it, that I thought I had a pretty good Idea of it, and now at ſupper, requeſted the gentlemen to tell me all they knew and thought worth notice relating to it, which they accordingly did. I obſerved that in many things they all agreed, in ſome things they were of different opinions, of all which I took particular notice. When they had told me all they knew, I made ſeveral queries to them concerning what I had read and heard of it, whether ſuch and ſuch a thing was true or not? and had their anſwers on every circumſtance. But as I have found by experience in my other travels, that very few obſerve nature's works with accuracy, or report the truth preciſely, I cannot now be entirely ſatisfied without ſeeing with my own eyes whenever 'tis in my power, Accordingly the next morning, being the 13th of *Auguſt*, at break of day, I ſet out for the Fall. The commandant had given orders to two of the Officers of the Fort to go with me and ſhew me every thing, and alſo ſent by them an order to Monſr. *Jonqueire*, who had liv'd ten years by the carrying-place, and

M   knew

knew every thing worth notice of the Fall, better than any other perſon, to go with me, and ſhew and tell me whatever he knew. A little before we came to the carrying-place, the water of *Niagara* River grew ſo rapid, that four men in a light birch canoe, had much difficulty to get up thither. Canoes can go half a league above the beginning of the carrying-place, tho' they muſt work againſt a water extremely rapid ; but higher up it is quite impoſſible, the whole courſe of the water for two leagues and a half up to the great Fall, being a ſeries of ſmaller Falls, one under another, in which the greateſt canoe or Battoe would in a moment be turn'd upſide down. We went aſhore therefore, and walk'd over the carrying-place, having beſides the high and ſteep ſide of the river, two great hills to aſcend one above the other. Here on the carrying-place I ſaw above 200 *Indians*, moſt of them belonging to the *Six Nations*, buſy in carrying packs of furs, chiefly of deer and bear, over the carrying-place. You would be ſurpriz'd to ſee what abundance of theſe things are brought every day over this place. An *Indian* gets 20 pence for ever pack he carries over, the diſtance being three leagues. Half an hour paſt 10 in the morning we came to the great Fall, which I found as follows. to the river (or rather ſtrait,)runs here from S. S. E. to N. N. W and the rocks of the great

Fall

Fall croſſes it, not in a right line; but form-
ing almoſt the figure of a ſemicircle or horſe
ſhoe. Above the Fall, in the middle of the
river is an iſland, lying alſo S. S. E. and
N. N. W. or parallel with the ſides of the
river; its length is about 7 or 8 french arpents
(an arpent being 180 feet.) the lower end of
this Iſland is juſt at the perpendicular edge of
the Fall. On both ſides of this iſland runs all
the water that comes from the lakes of *Canada*,
viz. Lake *Superior*, lake *Miſchigan*, lake
Huron, and lake *Erie*, which you know are
rather ſmall ſeas than lakes, and have beſides
a great many large rivers that empty their
water in them, of which the greateſt part comes
down this *Niagara* Fall. Before the water
comes to this iſland, it runs but ſlowly, com-
par'd with its motion when it approaches
the iſland, where it grows the moſt rapid
water in the World, runing with a ſurprizing
ſwiftneſs before it comes to the Fall; it is
quite white, and in many places is thrown
high up into the air! The greateſt and ſtrongeſt
battoes would here in a moment be turn'd
over and over. The water that goes down on
the weſt ſide of the iſland, is more rapid, in
greater abundance, whiter, and ſeems almoſt
to outdo an arrow in ſwiftneſs. When you are
at the Fall, and look up the river, you may
ſee, that the river above the Fall is every
where exceeding ſteep, almoſt as the ſide of a

M 2   hill

hill. When all this water comes to the very Fall, there it throws itself down perpendicular! It is beyond all belief the surprize when you see this! I cannot with words express how amazing it is! You cannot see it without being quite terrified; to behold so vast a quantity of water falling headlong from a surprising height! I doubt not but you have a desire to learn the exact height of this great Fall. Father *Hennepin*, supposes it 600 Feet perpendicular; but he has gained little credit in *Canada*; the name of honour they give him there, is *un grand Menteur*, or *The great Liar*; he writes of what he saw in places where he never was. 'tis true he saw this Fall: but as it is the way of some travellers to magnify every thing, so has he done with regard to the fall of *Niagara*. This humour of travellers, has occasioned me many disappointments in my travels, having seldom been so happy as to find the wonderful things that had been related by others. For my part, who am not fond of the *Marvellous*, I like to see things just as they are, and so to relate them. Since Father *Hennepin's* time. this Fall by all the accounts that have been given of it, has grown less and less; and those who have measur'd it with mathematical instruments find the perpendicular fall of the water to be exactly 137 feet. Monsr. *Morandrier*, the king's engineer in

Canada,

Canada, affured me, and gave it me alfo under
his hand, that 137 Feet was precifely the
height of it; and all the *French* Gentlemen
that were prefent with me at the Fall, did
agree with him, without the leaft contradiction:
it is true, thofe who have try'd to meafure it
with a line, find it fometimes 140, fometimes
150 feet, and fometimes more; but the reafon
is, it cannot that way be meafured with any
certainty, the water carrying away the
Line.——When the water is come down to
the bottom of the rock of the Fall, it jumps
back to a very great heighth in the air; in
other places it is white as milk or fnow; and
all in motion like a boiling chaldron.——You
may remember, to what a great diftance *He-*
nepin fays the noife of this great Fall may be
heard. All the gentlemen who were with
me, agreed, that the fartheft one can hear it,
is 15 leagues, and that very feldom. When
the air is quite calm, you can hear it to *Nia-*
gara Fort; but feldom at other times, becaufe
when the wind blows, the waves of Lake
Ontario make too much noife there againft
the Shore.——They inform'd me, that when
they hear at the Fort the noife of the Fall,
louder than ordinary, they are fure a North
Eaft Wind will follow, which never fails:
this feems wonderful, as the Fall is South Weft
from the Fort: and one would imagine it to
be rather a fign of a contrary wind. Sometimes,

times, 'tis said, the Fall makes a much greater
noise than at other times ; and this is look'd upon as a certain mark of approaching bad weather, or rain ; the *Indians* here hold it always
for a sure sign. When I was there, it did not
make an extraordinary great noise : just by
the Fall, we could easily hear what each other
said, without speaking much louder than common when conversing in other places. I do
not know how others have found so great a
noise here, perhaps it was at certain times,
as abovementioned. From the Place where
the water falls, there rise abundance of vapours,
like the greatest and thickest smoak, sometimes more, sometimes less : these vapours
rise high in the air when it is calm, but are
dispers'd by the wind when it blows hard.
If you go nigh to this vapour or fog, or if
the wind blows it on you, it is so penetrat-
ing, that in a few minutes you will be as wet
as if you had been under water. I got two
young *Frenchmen* to go down, to bring me
from the side of the Fall at the bottom, some
of each of the several kinds of herbs, stones
and shells they should find there ; they returned in a few minutes, and I really thought
they had fallen into the water : they were
obliged to strip themselves quite naked, and
hang their clothes in the sun to dry. When
you are on the other East side of the Lake
Ontario, a great many leagues from the Fall,
you

you may, every clear and calm morning fee
the vapours of the Fall rifing in the air ; you
would think all the woods thereabouts were fet
on fire by the *Indians,* fo great is the apparent
fmoak. In the fame manner you may fee it on
the Weft fide of the lake *Erie,* a great many
leagues off.

Several of the *French* gentlemen told me,
that when birds come flying into this fog or
fmoak of the fall, they fall down and perifh in
the Water ; either becaufe their wings are become wet, or that the noife of the fall aftonifh-
es them, and they know not were to go in the
Dark : but others were of opinion, that
feldom or never any bird perifhes there in that
manner ; becaufe, as they all agreed, among
the abundance of birds found dead below the
fall, there are no other forts then fuch as live
and fwim frequently in the water ; as fwans,
geefe, ducks, water-hens, teal, and the like.
And very often great flocks of them are feen
going to deftruction in this manner : they fwim
in the river above the fall, and fo are carried
down lower and lower by the water, and as
water-fowl commonly take great delight in
being carry'd with the ftream, fo here they in-
dulge themfelves in enjoying this pleafure fo
long, till the fwiftnefs of the water becomes fo
great, that 'tis no longer poffible for them to
rife, but they are driven down the precipice,
and perifh. They are obferv'd when they
draw

draw nigh the fall, to endeavour with all their might, to take wing and leave the water, but they cannot. In the months of *September* and *October*, fuch abundant quantities of dead waterfowl are found every morning below the Fall, on the fhore, that the garrifon of the fort for a long time live chiefly upon them; befides the fowl, they find alfo feveral forts of dead fifh, alfo deer, bears, aud other animals which have tried to crofs the water above the fall; the larger animals are generally found broken to pieces. Juft below the fall the water is not rapid, but goes all in circles and whirls like a boiling pot; which however doth not hinder the *Indians* going upon it in fmall canoes a fifhing; but a little lower begins the fmaller fall. When you are above the fall, and look down, your head begins to turn: the *French* who have been here 100 times, will feldom venture to look down, without at the fame time keeping faft hold of fome tree with one hand.

It was formerly thought impoffible for any body living to come at the Ifland that is in the middle of the fall: but an accident that happen'd 12 years ago, or thereabouts, made it appear otherwife. The hiftory is this. Two *Indians* of the *Six Nations* went out from *Niagara* fort, to hunt upon an ifland that is in the middle of the river, or ftrait, above the great fall, on which there ufed to be abundance of deer. They took fome *French* brandy with
them

them, from the fort, which they tafted feveral
times as they were going over the carrying
place; and when they were in the canoe,
they took now and then a dram, and fo went
along up the ftrait towards the Ifland where
they propos'd to hunt; but growing fleepy,
they laid themfelves down in the canoe, which
getting loofe drove back with the ftream, farther and farther down till it came nigh that
ifland that is in the middle of the fall. Here
one of them, awakened by the noife of the fall.
cries out to the other, that they were gone!
yet they try'd if poffible to favelife. This ifland
was nigheft, and with much working they got
on fhore there. At firft they were glad; but
when they had confider'd every thing, they
thought themfelves hardly in a better ftate
than if they had gone down the fall, fince they
had now no other choice, than either to throw
themfelves down the fame, or to perifh with
hunger. But hard neceffity put them on in-
vention. At the lower end of the ifland the
rock is perpendicular, and no water is running
there. This ifland has plenty of wood, they
went to work directly and made a ladder or
fhrouds of the bark of lindentree, (which is
very tough and ftrong,) fo long 'till they
could with it reach the water below ; one end
of this bark ladder they tied faft to a great
tree that grew at the fide of the rock a-
bove the fall, and let the other end down

N   to

to the water. So they went down along
their new-invented ftairs, and when they came
to the bottom in the middle of the fall,
they refted a little ; and as the water next
below the fall is not rapid, as beforementi-
oned, they threw themfelves out into it,
thinking to fwim on fhore. I have faid before, that one part of the fall is on one fide
of the ifland, the other on the other fide.
Hence it is, that the waters of the two cataracts running againft each other, turn back
againft the rock that is juft under the ifland.
Therefore, hardly had the *Indians* began to
fwim, before the waves of the eddy threw
them with violence againft the rock from
whence they came. They tried it feveral
times, but at laft grew weary ; and being
often thrown againft the rock they were
much bruis'd, and the skin of their bodies
torn in many places. So they were oblig'd
to climb up their ftairs again to the ifland, not
knowing what to do. After fome time they
perceived *Indians* on the fhore, to whom they
cried out. Thefe faw and pity'd them, but
gave them little hopes of help : yet they made
hafte down to the fort, and told the comman-
der where two of their brethren were. He
perfuaded them to try all poffible means of
relieving the two poor *Indians* ; and it was
done in this manner. The water that runs on
the eaft fide of this ifland is fhallow, efpecially

a

a little above the iſland towards the eaſtern
ſhore. The commandant cauſed poles to be
made and pointed with iron: two *Indians*
determined to walk to this iſland by the
help of theſe poles, to ſave the other poor
creatures, or periſh themſelves. They took
leave of all their friends as if they were going
to death. Each had two ſuch poles in his
hands, to ſet againſt the bottom of the ſtream,
to keep them ſteady. So they went and got
to the iſland, and having given poles to the
two poor *Indians* there, they all returned ſafely
to the main. Thoſe two *Indians* who in the
above mentioned manner were firſt brought to
this iſland, are yet alive. They were nine
days on the iſland, and almoſt ſtarved to death.*
—Now ſince the way to this iſland has been
found, the *Indians* go there often to kill deer,
which having tried to croſs the river above the
fall, were driven upon the iſland by the
ſtream: but if the King of *France* would give
me all *Canada*, I would not venture to go
to this iſland; and were you to ſee it, Sir, I
am ſure you would have the ſame ſentiment.
On the weſt ſide of this iſland are ſome ſmall
iſlands or rocks of no conſequence. The eaſt

* Theſe *Indians* had better fortune than 10 or 12 *Utowawa's*
who attempting to eſcape here the purſuit of their Enemies
of the *Six Nations*, were carried down the Cataract, by the
violence of the ſtream and every one periſhed.——No part
even of their Canoe being ever ſeen again.

ſide

fide of the river is nearly perpendicular, the
weft fide more floping. In former times a
part of the rock at the Fall which is on the
weft fide of the ifland, hung over in fuch a
manner, that the water which fell perpendi-
cularly from it, left a vacancy below, fo that
people could go under between the rock and
the water; but the prominent part fome years
fince broke off and fell down; fo that there
is now no poffibility of going between the
falling water and the rock, as the water now
runs clofe to it all the way down.——The
breadth of the Fall, as it runs into a femicircle,
is reckon'd to be about 6 Arpents. The ifland
is in the middle of the Fall, and from it to
each fide is almoft the fame breadth: the
breadth of the ifland at its lower end is two
thirds of an Arpent, or thereabouts.——Below
the Fall in-the holes of the rocks, are great
plenty of Eels, which the *Indians* and *French*
catch with their hands without other means;
I fent down two *Indian* boys, who directly
came up with about twenty fine ones.——
Every day, when the Sun fhines, you fee here
from 10 o'clock in the morning to 2 in the
afternoon, below the Fall, and under you,
when you ftand at the fide over the Fall, a
glorious rainbow and fometimes two rainbows,
one within the other.

I was

I was fo happy to be at the Fall on a fine clear day, and it was with great delight I view'd this rainbow, which had almoft all the colours you fee in a rainbow in the air. The more vapours, the brighter and clearer is the rainbow. I faw it on the Eaft fide of the Fall in the bottom under the place where I ftood, but above the water. When the wind carries the vapours from that place, the rainbow is gone, but appears again as foon as new vapours come. From the Fall to the landing above the Fall, where the canoes from Lake *Erie* put on fhore, (or from the Fall to the upper end of the carrying-place) is half a mile. Lower the canoes dare not come, left they fhould be obliged to try the fate of the two *Indians*, and perhaps with lefs fuccefs.—— They have often found below the Fall pieces of human bodies, perhaps of drunken *Indians*, that have unhappily came down the Fall. I was told at *Ofwego*, that in *October*, or there-abouts, fuch plenty of feathers are to be found here below the Fall, that a man in a days time can gather enough of them for feveral beds, which feathers they faid came off the birds kill'd at the Fall. I ask'd the *French*, if this was true? They told me they had never feen any fuch thing; but that if the feathers were pick'd off the dead birds, there might be fuch a quantity. The *French* told me, they had often thrown whole great trees into

the

the water above, to fee them tumble down the Fall. They went down with furprifing fwiftnefs, but could never be feen afterwards; whence it was thought there was a bottomlefs deep or abyfs juft under the Fall. I am alfo of Opinion, that there muft be a vaft deep here; yet I think if they had watched very well, they might have found the trees at fome diftance below the Fall. The rock of the Fall confifts of a grey limeftone.

Here you have, Sir, a fhort but exact defcription of this famous *Niagara* cataract : you may depend on the truth of what I write. You muft excufe me if you find in my acccount, no extravagant wonders. I cannot make nature otherwife than I find it. I had rather it fhould be faid of me in time to come, that I related things as they were, and that all is found to agree with my Defcription; than to be efteem'd a falfe Relater. I have feen fome other things in this my journey, an account of which I know would gratify your curiofity; but time at prefent will not permit me to write more; and I hope fhortly to fee you. I am, &c.

PETER KALM.

F I N I S.

Printed in the United States
By Bookmasters